Christian's Climb

ISBN 978-0-6151-8379-4

First Paperback Edition, December 2007

Dedicated to Ray and Paul, my beloved children. May you persevere through this world with understanding.

Love, Mommy

TABLE OF CONTENTS

Part 2: The Demons

Part 3: The World

Part 4: The Passage

Part 1: The Backpack

Chapter 1: "Lock-Down"
"He that will save his life shall lose it'" [Mark 8:35]

Rodney Middleton stood still, numbly, as the guard frisked him down.

"Any weapons, drugs, or contraband?" the guard asked.

"No, man," returned Rodney.

"Legs apart," the guard drilled. With a few more smacks to the legs, Rodney was done and put in line with seven other kids who had managed to find their way to Juvie. The jail itself wasn't going to be that bad, Rodney had heard. No picnic, either, though. Just a speedbump in his road. In two months he'd be right back out there, doing what he did best. A kid had to make money, and, besides, he wasn't really hurting anyone else, was he? *Think of it as a long vacation,* he told himself. "I'm still in control," he stammered under his breath.

After Rodney sat for an hour in the waiting room, it was his turn in the examining room. That doctor was OK. He told Rodney his body was doing fine.

Then came the IQ test. *What in the heck do they need an IQ test for?* Rodney wondered to himself. *Probably to see who to keep their eye on. . . who's smart enough to make it out of here.*

Hmm. . . no dinner tonight. I must've missed it, Rodney told his growling stomach. "Musta missed supper," Rodney casually announced to a red-haired kid who had been ten minutes behind him in the whole production.

"Ya, musta," the kid vaguely agreed.

Last in the "tour" came the sleeping barracks. He knew that with such an empty rec room and nothing else to do, a lot of time was going to be spent here.

"All right, all you lawbreakers, time for your first night in the Hard-Guy Hotel," boomed out a large, formidable guard with two night sticks that swung off his hips as he walked. Nobody dared answer. "Lights out." The metallic clank of locks echoed throughout the vast cell.

As Rodney lay on his bed covered with a thin, gray blanket and worn sheets smelling of nothing but bleach, his thoughts began to pick up speed, only in a disturbing way. It was like an old, brakeless race car that was accelerating. As his eyes began to droop, the reckless vehicle was careening through the streets while its driver could do nothing more than hold on. It was more than a little frightening. He had no control.

Hours earlier, little here had mattered. Now, it was all about the squealing of tires, the violent weaving in and out of streets during what could be the longest night of his life. His heavy lids came up for air one final time and then slammed shut.

Chapter 2: "Thy Kingdom Come, Thy Will Be Done"
'What shall I do?" [Acts 16:30-31]

Floating somewhere between deep sleep and the kind of sleep in which we sometimes sleeptalk or, even worse, sleepwalk or *sleepdrive*, Rodney saw the shape of a body zipping through the night. It nearly got hit running across the street, by a speeding black car. Without even missing a beat, the dream shape kept running, pointlessly darting to the left, to the right, in panicked bursts of adrenaline. The shape—a kid--, now back on the sidewalk, ran with everything he had, for three more city blocks, driven by some unseen force, but aimlessly. Then nearing the end of the long, frantic dash, he began losing steam, and quickly.

He slowed and then stopped, hands on his knees to catch his breath. Anybody could see he was mess, a real mess: hood up, a charcoal-gray sweatshirt with grime on the pocket, "the look" complete with large rips in baggie, black jeans. He gripped a raggedy, old book in his hand, and—strangest of all—he had something huge on his back, a massive backpack of some sort.

A wanderer, a transient, a homeless kid, Rodney thought. *He's younger than me, too.*

Panting and wobbly, the boy fought to adjust his carry-all under its extreme weight.

"What you got in there. . . a dead body or somethin'?" a pedestrian—or was it a mugger?-- coming at him joked.

There was no response.

The pedestrian continued to stare.

"Naw," the boy decided to reply. Measuring his next words very, very slowly, he said, "It's my *horror*."

"Huh? Your *horror*? What's that supposed to mean?" The streetlight flickered overhead. With arms crossed, the pedestrian leaned against the lamppost, which had been bent and crimped two feet up, as if it had been struck by one of those heavy, municipal garbage trucks while backing up.

"Oh, it's just the pieces of life I've picked up here and there. . . from day after day . . . You've got one too, only you don't know it," the kid answered cryptically.

The pedestrian paused and stroked his chin. Irritated now, he moved away from the lamppost and demanded, "What are you saying? I ain't got no pack like that! Come on now, what is it? What *is* it?" A rushed passerby on the street uncaringly knocked into him but kept going.

"It's all my sin, all my sin!" cried the boy with the pack. "I can't deal with it anymore." He waited for a moment, and then finished: "But at least I can see it, and that's the first step to getting rid of it. And I *will* someday, too, just you watch me!"

"Listen," blurted the guy, moving in closer, "I know we'ze both crazies to be walkin' in the dark 'round this section a' town, but you gotta know better than to keep goin' around with something that's *that* heavy. Just plain drop it; drop it *now*!"

"I can't," whispered the boy, "not just yet." He looked down at the steaming sewer and then back up to the confused eyes of the guy.

"But a friend told me to read this, because it would help get the thing off," the boy explained, lifting his book for a shot of lamplight.

"Get it off?. . . It's not *glued* on your back, is it?" protested the guy. He reached around to the boy's back and tried to pull it off.

But, inexplicably, the pack wasn't going anywhere. It burned the guy's fingers, so that he jolted back in the air like someone who had touched an exposed wire.

The guy, then the boy, examined the fingertips; they *did* appear singed, slightly. "What is this?!" cried the pedestrian, backing off some steps.

The two just stood there checking each other out, under the flashes of light from the broken, neglected source.

"OK, then, go ahead and read the book!" the guy challenged, growing more impatient.

The boy slowly opened it near the back cover. He studied it for a few seconds, as if it were hard work, and then let out the most tortured, terrifying cry.

"Says here we're all gonna die!"

"What??" the guy exploded. "Show me!" He snatched the book right out of the kid's hands. "*Where* does it say *that*?" he asked, now noticeably troubled.

"Right here, right here!" the boy exclaimed, his right forefinger shaking along the lines. "It says fire's gonna rain down on this town from heaven and we're all gonna die!"

"No, can't be," the guy said slowly, thinking. "You're messed in the head. And now you're trying to mess with me! Get away from me, you creep!" He shook his head a couple times and walked off.

"Kill yourself with that load if I care!" he hollered as he turned his head back, far off down the street.

And with that, the kid spun around and bolted back into the night, only this time with a direction in mind.

Chapter 3: "Don't Even Go There"
"Fly from the wrath to come." [Matthew 3:7]

The boy with the pack sped home, staggering and weeping all the way. *Grandpa used to say "Jesus wept,"* he thought to himself, hot tears streaming down his face. Block after dirty block, he pounded the pavement in worn-out sneakers. Then, there it was, his mother's house, 13 Freewill Avenue, Deastrukshun: a shaky, wooden rowhouse on the West End, with peeling paint. He would beg them to hear him, but he wondered if they would listen any better than that guy had.

Ascending the rickety steps, he strained to manage the awful pounds on his back and entered the door with difficulty. Right away, his mother and brother saw his distress and encircled him at the kitchen table. "What's happened, Chris?" they asked with V-ed eyebrows, his mother putting down her cigarette.

He didn't even care about having nearly been mowed down by a car. "Mom, you gotta get outta here! You gotta get out now! We're gonna die! We're *all* gonna die!"

"What in God's name is going on? What's wrong!?" his mother screamed.

"It says here, Ma, right here in the Bible Grandpa left under his bed. I read it tonight. It says that the city's going to be destroyed-- in a ball of flame! All of us! Nobody's going to be able to escape! We gotta go!" Chris exerted again.

"Oh, Christian Michael, calm down! That's not meant to be taken word for word; it's just in there to. . . to *scare* people." She took a puff on her cigarette, then added with a sneer, "If I had thought you were going to make a mountain out of a molehill I never would've allowed you to go snooping in your grandfather's room!"

"But Mom!" Chris shouted. "You don't know. It's the truth! It's the truth! Every word of it. . . Grandpa said so when he was dyin' in his bed! I remember!"

"Listen here," she intoned, grappling for steadiness, "I don't want to hear none of that garbage!"

The words of denial impacted painfully and surprisingly, like the unexpected ring of a phone right against the eardrum. Chris looked at her, unable to combat the awful thud of no.

Then, gentler, she reasoned, "You're all stressed out from school and that new job you took on, besides all them hours worryin' 'bout Grandpa. You've been through a lot, 'pecially with your father leavin' and all, but let's not even go there. . .

"It's just too much for you. . . too much for your mind, Baby. . ." She paused, reflecting.

"Besides, go where? We got no place else to go! We probably don't even have *this place* for much longer. I don't want you goin' nowhere."

Her voice grew quieter and softer then, admonishing him while grinding out the cigarette. "Chris, honey, I'm sorry. . just go to sleep now. Things'll be better tomorrow." She suggested this weakly, her pitch rising as if she were asking a question.

Chris brushed off the awkward stare from his brother.

The little family "chat" being over, Chris put his Bible back into his pants pocket, climbed the stairs to his room, and fell face-first, exhausted, into bed with the pack still on.

Sleep didn't come, though, not really. He tossed rampantly, wrapping himself tighter and tighter into a hot, sweaty sea of sheets. "No, no!" he yelled out repeatedly.

Tomorrow would come, but Mom had lied. It would come with no relief in Chris's churning, strangling thoughts.

Chapter 4: "Evan's Light"
"Do you see yonder shining light?" [Psalms 119:105; 2 Peter 1:19]

About 5:30 AM, Chris woke with a start, straight up in bed. Throwing the covers aside, he ran to the window to see the condition of the city, thinking he might see firebolts streaming down from Heaven, people scattering everywhere. But no. What he saw was simply a man, sitting, no-- almost relaxing, on the front stoop of the Smith's house across the street.

Chris jerked the window open on its dilapidated frame and jutted his head out. "Who are you?" he yelled, but not so loudly as to wake up their mean, old next-door neighbor. "And what are you doing?"

Neglecting the first question, the mysterious stranger answered back flatly, "I was sent to help somebody, so I'm waiting here for him." He tapped a long cane on the Smith's porch.

"No! You've got to go! The City is about to be--" Chris was yelling for real now, despite his image of the neighbor with the baseball bat.

Cutting Chris off in mid-sentence, the stranger said, "destroyed." Chris just stared in amazement, jaw dropped.

"How'd you know?" cried Chris. *How could this man know?* No one else so far had known, or even cared for that matter. In fact, they had pretty much acted as if he were insane.

"Come on down here, and we'll talk," spoke the man, calmly.

Although talking to a complete stranger before dawn with no other people around was not exactly on Chris' list of known safe behaviors, his curiosity and anxiety got the best of him. Without even changing clothes from the day before, he bound down the stairs, tripping over his brother's discarded toys and what-have-you.

He ran across the street to where the man with the cane was sitting. "How'd you know?" he repeated, not even sitting down.

"I know," said the man, "same way you know. . ." He motioned for Chris to sit down and then turned his head sideways, speaking within just inches of the boy's face, in hushed tones.

"Now, listen, young man," he said, "You can't just run off in any direction; you've got to go the proper way."

"Proper way? You mean to tell me there's a right way? I just gotta get out 'a the city, right?" Chris was waiting for an answer.

"I'm afraid it's going to hit more than this city. . ." said the man, trying to keep his voice down, and sadly. He slowly moved his cane back and forth over an open hand, like someone playing a violin with no sound.

". . .But I bring you good news. There's a way to avoid it— one way."

He bore directly into Chris's eyes. Then his lips whispered, "Come with me. I will show you The Way."

"OK," said Chris, as he aligned his backpack more squarely. For some reason, it momentarily felt lighter. "Let's go," he said, with a bit of relief.

*   *   *

So the two got up and walked off, the man just fine without the cane. *That's weird,* mumbled Chris to himself.

The stranger and the boy walked several city blocks, as the rowhouses disappeared into sooty, desolate factories, and the sooty, desolate factories disappeared into farms that were spread out farther and farther. The two were way outside town now, but Chris couldn't remember ever having seen this area before.

He had to reposition his pack several times. The stranger never offered to take Chris' pack, and Chris never asked him. His energy was wearing thin. He sat down by the side of the road, near a broken fence post, releasing four, long, labored breaths. His traveling companion, not winded or tired, merely stood by Chris's feet, waiting.

Chris' head drooped. For a moment there, he thought he could actually drift into sleep. But the man gave his foot a tap with the cane. "There," he said, "look there." He pointed off into the distance.

Across a cornfield that had been partially harvested was a large, old gate in the fence. A hazy, warm light was

shining all around it. Chris looked at it, and an aura of
good feeling surrounded him. But then the familiar surge
of fear quickly replaced it. It was like when you see a
random five dollar bill lying on the ground and then
suddenly it is blown out of reach.

"Now, my boy," the stranger spoke, jarring Chris
back to reality, "I direct you to that gate. Seek The Light
behind it. That's all you have to do, and you will be safe
forever."

Chris could barely focus on the man. All he seemed
to hear was "gate." Lugging the horrible weight of his
backpack, he got up and sprinted through the dry, scratchy
corn shafts. It wouldn't be too far, an easy couple hundred
feet. He ran toward the light, building momentum.

"I'll see you there myself, someday," trailed the
stranger's voice. Chris didn't notice when the man
vanished.

I can do this, thought Chris, *piece of cake.* And
although it was a clear, lovely day, with safety lying just
steps away, things weren't going to be that easy . . .

Chapter 5: Obie and Ply
"No, not I, because I have laid my hand to the plow."
[Luke 9:62]

A boy named Obie and his friend, Ply, came charging at
Chris from the side. Chris knew these two kids from
school. Obie was an obstinate and highly negative sort,
never obeying teachers, always wanting to defy others'
suggestions, and, in general, opposing every request that
came his way. Ply, on the other hand, was just the
opposite, a kid who went along with the crowd and folded
easily under pressure: weak-willed and pliable, never

standing up for himself. Ply and Obie made the perfect pair, though, because for whatever Obie insisted, Ply would always agree with.

It's no surprise, then, that Obie had been the one who decided to talk to Chris when they first saw him sitting by the fence post.

"Hey," shouted Obie, "Wait up! Where are you goin'? Why are you so far outta the city?"

"I'm trying to escape!" yelled Chris, hardly slowing down at all.

"What? Escape from *what*? Hey, wait a minute!" shouted Obie, even more forcefully.

Frustrated by this hindrance, Chris did stop to address it. "Why aren't you at school? You two skip all the time!"

Then, as he began to explain why he was running away, he started to feel badly that he had almost not stopped to tell them, two kids he had been with since kindergarten. *Certainly they deserve to be saved too*, he thought.

Chris talked to them of his grandfather's cherished book, the chilling prediction, the promise of the gate's light. Obie listened with obvious contempt, continually looking away.

Chris begged Obie and Ply to come. But Obie crossed his arms in front of himself. "Looks like you got a lot on your back--a lot 'a *issues*, that is!. . . Did a bum just give you his suitcase!?" he jeered in his classic bully style.

This was good for one wimpy chuckle out of Ply.

"As for me, I'm not goin' nowhere," he said, looking Chris squarely in the eye, as if to provoke him.

"Why? You're gonna be killed, I tell you!"

"Nope," continued Obie. "Even if I did b'lieve your dumb ideas, my pop's farm is here, and we're here to stay. Come wind, rain, or shine, we're here to stay, just like we did for generations. We is country folk through and through, right, Ply?" He looked to Ply for confirmation, and Ply nodded his head.

"Besides, 'taint nothing special 'bout that gate," added Obie. "Turn back, Chris. You got some fool-headed hunkerins, that's for sure!"

Ply looked sheepishly at the worry stretched across Chris's face.

Words started to slip out of Ply's mouth, but Obie was quick to cut him off. "No, no, no, I said we're doin' things *my* way, and goin' off with this nut ain't part o' the plan!"

After a moment, Obie added, smiling, "You couldn't drag us off this property with a crane."

"OK, have it your way," said Chris with ill will, "but you're gonna regret it." He started to go again.

"*See* ya! See ya when Hell freezes over!" Obie shouted with corresponding derision.

Obie and Ply were mumbling something to themselves. Ply looked as if he may have wanted to follow, but Obie was holding him back.

Chp. 6 "The Slew"

"There shall be no more crying, nor sorrow; for He that is owner of the place will wipe all tears from your eyes." *[Revelation 21:4]*

The cornstalks bristled against Chris's legs. When he got to the field's other end, he saw the shimmering gate up close. Just to the left of it, nailed to an old fence rail, was a wooden sign, painted in sloppy, capital red letters: "THE SLEW." Under that, it read "This way" and had an arrow.

So this is the way to The Slew, Chris thought excitedly. He had heard of this place before! There were lots of rumors about what went on there. It was where the older, "cool" but "bad" crowd hung out. The sign and the stories were more than enough to prick his interest. Ignoring the gate and the instructions from the man with the cane, Chris turned and proceeded.

There was an opening in the fence where a path started. Chris was soon surrounded by large saplings. With the leaves at the treetops shading the path, there wasn't much light in there. There was only a brooding gloom.

As he walked on, a broken beer bottle caught Chris's attention, and then another and another. Not too long afterwards, the path widened quickly until the boy found himself entering a great dirt circle, the perfect meeting place. *Wild parties,* said Chris to himself. *This is it!* He turned around, holding his arms out, spinning faster and faster with glee.

Then Chris began to walk around the clearing's perimeter, just to be able to say he'd done it, if he ever got back to his city; that is, if the prediction hadn't come true.

Something shiny caught his eye. It was nearer to the inside of the circle, so he went to inspect it. It looked like a thin piece of silver metal. Carefully, he lifted it out of the dirt. *A CD, a broken CD,* he thought. *Musta been from a long time ago.*

Just then, Chris felt his feet begin to slide. He looked down at his sneakers and saw that they were covered in mud. He jumped to the left, but again, he was in mud. He jumped to the right, but that too was muddy, even muddier. In fact, the mud was a soup, and Chris was knee deep now. *Oh no, it's a swamp!* he yelled inside himself. Pulling one leg up with the weight of the clinging muck, he lost his balance because of the backpack, and he fell backwards from the standing leg.

With his body, all except for one arm, now immersed in mud, he began to panic. He tried to move back to where the mud was shallower, but his feet couldn't find firm ground. Thrashing, he tried to release the pack from his shoulders, but the mud was so thick it wouldn't budge even if it could have.

Perhaps ten minutes elapsed. The struggle felt like when you try to move your legs underwater, only the water was more like cement. As he bobbed up and down, slowly, futilely, the mud progressed higher and higher up his body and eventually over his mouth and nose. In vain, he screamed, "Help! Help!" But he knew he was kidding himself.

On about the tenth lunge upward, he made the terrible realization that he was going to drown in this quicksand-like mire, with no one ever knowing. (Obviously, no popularity would ever come of being here.) It was ironic, he thought, as time stood still for a millisecond: just a foot away was dry land. A million thoughts and images raced through his frontal lobe. *Maybe this is how that teenage girl mysteriously died a few years back. Maybe this is why some kids' parents forbade them to go. . . .*

On the way down from that upward stroke, he actually went under all the way. He was able to come up for air, but when he slipped below again, this time it was for good. A few bubbles of CO_2 slowly emerged from the churned-up patch of ground, and nothing more.

Under the surface, Chris was beyond terror; it was the saddest of leaden resignations. *I'm going to die,* he said internally, *I'm done for.* Fleetingly, the vision of his grandfather's arms came to him, the arms that had saved him so many times before. *Grandfather. . . I miss him so much. But he's dead. . . and now so am I. . .*

And with those words, it was just about over. He could not move at all.

* * *

Just then, Chris felt something grab him under the shoulder. It was a hook of some kind, pulling him, yanking him in quick bursts. Somebody was rescuing him! He opened his eyes and the thick slime filled them. He was jerked with several more brisk movements and then dragged onto the edge of the bog.

Chris lay on his back panting, then wiped his sludge-covered, gritty eyes. He made out someone standing before him: it appeared to be the messenger-man from before.

"You!" Chris screamed. "You saved me!" Chris could see that it had been the man's cane that had been the life-saving equipment.

"I told you to go to the Light!" said the man in an upset voice.

"I know, I know!" rejoined Chris. "It's just that this place, this place; it drew me in."

"You've got to stay on the correct path, Chris!" exclaimed the man. Then, more fatherly, he urged, "You've got to stay on the straight and narrow. Don't be lured this way and that. Stay focused on the goal. And don't let your responses to difficulties overwhelm you."

"I can never thank you enough, mister; I apologize. I know what you told me, and I'm sorry I let you down. I won't do it again," promised Chris, feeling a little disgusted with himself.

Chris stood up and scraped off as much mud as he could. They walked back the way Chris had come, speaking nothing, the disappointment on the man's face all too apparent.

Chapter 7 "Unwanted Friends"

"The Lord says, 'Strive to enter in at the strait gate.'"
[Luke 13:24]

Chris and the mysterious man had reached the gleaming gate again. "By the way," said Chris, warming up to him through a great deal of natural gratitude, "I'm Chris."

"I know; and I'm Evan," he said, disappearing. He had slipped right through Chris's fingers-- again.

But wait! Chris said inaudibly. *I had some questions for you!*

Chris felt exasperated, though lucky that he had survived such a close call. *"Evan" plus "angel" equals "Evangel"* he said to himself, intrigued by the overlap of syllables. *It's like the word Evangelist,* he decided, remembering his mother having used this term in reference to a Christian missionary who had once come to their door.

* * *

His mind snapped back to the present. Here at the gate he suddenly saw a large, young adult, looking down and shuffling money, lots of it. His designer pants were in fact stuffed with money. He looked sharp, with his expensive leather shoes and jacket. He had spiked, neatly gelled hair, and the smell of cologne wafting off him was strong. Chris was probably going to have to talk to this guy in order to pass through the gate.

"Hi," Chris said as he leaned over, reaching for the latch.

The guy, quickly cramming the wad of cash into his pocket, put his hand on Chris' forearm. "Hey, not so fast, buddy."

They looked at each other confrontationally, then the young man's expression softened. Charismatically, he said, "I was wondering if you could give me directions into the next city— Deastrukshun."

Chris was leery of this guy already, because he just seemed too forward, too smooth, too perfect. *Not a hair out of place, but . . .* It was exactly like the impression you have when you meet someone who makes you feel instantly uncomfortable, though you have no idea why.

"Uhh," sputtered Chris, trying to think of how to give the directions in the fewest possible words. "Just keep goin' west from here. It's about fifteen miles. Follow the sun and you should be there before sundown. It's afternoon now, right?"

The guy glanced at his loose Rolex. "Quarter past twelve to be sure," he confirmed. He spoke in a slightly superior tone.

"OK, then, good luck," Chris said, trying to steer the conversation to an end, all the while hoping the guy's hand would release its grasp. But nothing doing; the guy was clearly stalling him. *What does he want from me?* Chris wondered.

Catching Chris' feeling, the guy relaxed his grip a little and explained, "Lucky I met you out here. Didn't think I'd see anybody. I was coming from the next city over, Reltivismville."

There was an awkward space of silence. Then the guy seemed to suddenly have the urge to make small talk. "Hey, pal, I was just wondering if you'd like to get in on a big-time deal I got going in Deastrukshun. I got some contacts there who want my stuff."

Chris was expressionless.

"We could go together; you could be my right-hand man. I got some excellent product this month. . . " he offered, with a note of pride. He looked at his other hand and bounced his thumb against one fingertip at a time, quickly, as if calculating something.

"As a matter of fact," spoke Chris assuredly, yet with a hint of annoyance, "I was just on my way from leavin' that place. I've lived there since I was a kid."

"Oh, ya, well . . ," said the young man suavely, apparently not someone used to taking no for an answer. He smiled a wide slit of a smile, full of perfect, glistening teeth. Chris thought he might even have eyeliner on, to make him look extra appealing. "Pick you up some nice threads," he suggested, vainly flicking the collar of his blazer in illustration.

Chris felt now that he was not only being detained, but accosted. He glared at the guy, and wasn't able to conceal his resentment. The muscle on one side of his nose automatically drew up, and his eyes narrowed in suspicion. The guy finally relinquished his hold entirely.

"Hey, I'm no sleezeball, man," said the young guy, "if that's what you're thinking. I got myself a legit business going, and I'm just offerin' you a piece of the pie. Anybody else'd jump at the chance. There'll be plenty a' other takers in your town. . . "

Christian considered whether he had hurt the person's feelings. "Sorry; didn't mean anything by it," he said, apologetically.

"No problem! A dude's got to be wise these days . . .watch out for them punches, eh?" The guy was waxing philosophical. "The world is tough, real tough. You got to be worldly, and you got to be wise. You got to take this world so it doesn't take you! See what I'm sayin'?"

"So, do you want ta go for it, or *not*, bud?" he demanded of Chris with finality. In the emphasis of the word "not," Chris sensed guile, slyness.

"Naw, I think I'll pass this time around , . . . but thanks for the offer," he said, glad to be able to think quickly on his feet.

"Major profit margin," the guy pushed, in hopes that Chris might reconsider.

Chris just shook his head.

"Got it," said the guy, mentally brushing off the refusal.

Chris again went for the latch, but it was rusty and wouldn't budge. He tried to work it up and down, to no avail.

Taking advantage of the problem, the guy wheedled, "Listen, you gave me the directions. Now, is there anything *I* can do for *you*, seein' as though you live back where I'm goin' to set up shop? I mean, we're bound to run into each other some day, and 'one hand washes the other,' ya know?"

"No, but thanks again, man," said Chris. He hated saying things twice.

"Sure, sure," returned the aggressive young guy. But his tone had completely changed. "Let me give you a tip, though, OK?" His sight was bearing down brutishly on Chris now. "I *know* you're runnin' away, man, because no city kid would be out here alone. And I know kids don't just run away for nothin'."

How many times did Mom warn me not to run away? Chris asked himself. A cloud of defeat floated over him.

Chris was feeling flushed now, regretting so many things. Why hadn't he tried just a little bit harder to get his mom to come with him? *Then at least she wouldn't be worried sick right now. . .*

"If you're in trouble," continued the guy's slick speech, "I got some help for you. It's my man: me and my guys call him 'Mr. Legality' because he's the best lawyer you'd ever want ta have. He's gotten me out of quite a few 'situations,' if you know what I mean. Good defense guy—possession, dealing, assault, you name it-- and likes to buy in return for services, so you don't have to scrape together a lot a' dough outa nowhere. He's over there in the next town, *my* town, about six miles that-a-way."

Pointing, the impeccably groomed conman was beaming now, feeling as though in imparting this advice he was doing Chris a great favor. "Just go to 66 Corporate Bend, Suite 13, and you'll find him there. He's your 'man in a jam,' we always say!"

Chris felt as if he was going to vomit. He didn't need that kind of help, nor had he ever.

Chp. 8 **"Shaken"**
"Here therefore he sweat, and did quake for fear."
[Hebrews 12:21]

The guy resumed counting his money, and Chris finally got the latch to move. It snapped up and Chris passed through, light flowing all around him and seeping into his skin, or so he imagined. He would be safe forever now. And he would live happily ever after. But that's not what really happened.

* * *

What really happened was this: yes, the guy resumed counting his money, but Chris hesitated and began to actually consider the tip; he was falling for the bait. He was oblivious that this worldly, street-wise guy (known as "Worldy Wiseman" to his partners in crime) was in fact rerouting him to a no-good colleague who would be even more twistedly persuasive. *'Man in a jam,'* eh?

Maybe his friend the lawyer could help my mom, imagined Chris. *Maybe he could help us get child support, or file for bankruptcy.* It was an attractive idea.

"OK, thanks, I'll go see him," Chris said to Wiseman. Turning so that the sun was to his right, Chris was going to head south now. *Six miles, six miles,* he repeated in his head, the gate out of sight, out of mind.

* * *

There was a road that went directly south, so convenient. He walked along slowly for what seemed more like ten miles or so, until he could see the outline of the tops of some buildings. *This must be it—the next city—Relativ-whatever he said!*

And Chris surmised right. There was a marquee posting the city's name and token phrase: "Reltivismville: Where Everything is Relative."

Chris walked on. His backpack continued to vex him. He flipped each strap upside down, hoping that the additional padding from where it had not worn down yet would alleviate his discomfort.

It was then that he saw an enormous, jagged fissure in the ground. It seemed to run for miles. Chris had an odd, sinking feeling, full of inexplicable dread. Thank goodness he didn't have to cross that crack.

"Sixty-six Corporate Bend, Suite 13," Chris kept saying aloud, hoping to brand the address into his memory. *Sixty-six Corporate Bend.*

A stoplight on the road blinked yellow, a warning for motorists to slow down upon entering the fine city. Chris crossed the street easily, as no cars or people were visible for miles.

The trick with the straps had failed, and the backpack was becoming particularly irksome now. It wasn't without several rest stops that Chris was able to go on.

"Sixty-six Corporate Bend," he said, again. The streets were strangely silent. He walked into an abandoned gas station and found a map.

Then Chris went down three streets, made a left, and a right. As he went, he still felt odd about the absence of people. Not a soul was present.

"Hmm, forty-six, forty-eight." He counted aloud as he progressed down the wide, barren street. *The numbers are going up, so I'll soon be there!*

* * *

Just at that moment, Chris heard a terrible splitting noise way off in the distance and felt the ground shake. The blast sent ripples that made his legs tremble. *Woah, what was THAT?* Chris's mind was scattering in all directions. With a second violent shudder, this one even more intense than the last, Chris could hear what sounded like a toppling of debris. Then, there were some additional aftershocks.

Although he was frantic, Chris continued to search for Number Sixty-Six Corporate Bend, and he did find it soon. An expensive-looking, gold-rimmed sign hung outside the tall edifice, listing several professionals' names and their credentials. And there it was all right, a name with the title "Attorney at Law" underneath. Chris glanced through the building's front window, but not a person was in sight.

Then, a third boom came, this one by far the worst: it knocked Chris off the steps before he could squeeze the door handle. *Oh, Dear God!* Chris's mind put the words together faster than electricity running down a cable. *Where are all the people?* Pulling himself off the ground, and examining a good-sized scrape on his leg, Chris realized what was happening. *It's an earthquake! That's why the city's deserted!*

All of a sudden, several small tremors pulsed through the land, and Chris saw the office building cave in on one side. He could hear many crashes off in the distance. A small crack began carving up the length of the street. *It's just a matter of time now,* thought Chris, *until I'm trapped.*

So Chris charged off in the opposite direction, running through countless twisting, turning streets. He was way overheated and parched; however, his strides kept lightning pace with his thoughts. *I hate that pusher for sending me here. I HATE him!!*

And in regard to the lawyer, Christian knew what his grandfather would have probably said about him and his "style" of operating: *a child playing at straws. . . a kid building a structure distorting gravity, amazing to see, but always about to collapse. . .*

An earthquake doesn't do that, came the next thought. *It doesn't bother with arguing; it tells it like it is. An earthquake levels everything.*

Chris stopped at a street corner. He looked at a sign on a shop. Apparently, before it was damaged, the sign had read:

"A.G. ODER & SLOAN—WASTE
MANAGEMENT
AND SCRAP METAL BUYER."

As a result of the quake, half of the letters, and the top and bottom of the "B," had shut off. Now it read:

"GODS LAWS R HUYER."

Christian ran and he ran until he was safely away. He was uphill from where he had felt the last vibrations. Having extricated himself from the danger zone, he was significantly "uphill" in his mood as well.

Chp. 9 "Counsel and Connections"

"Knock, and it shall be opened unto you." [Matthew 7:8]

The mood was absurdly short-lived. The city out of sight, Chris realized that he had completely lost his bearings. Disoriented and breathless, his head began to spin. He plunged to the ground, doubled over. "Where am I? Where am I?" he cried. He couldn't even remember where he was supposed to be going.

"You are now quite far from The Light; 'tis a pity."

Chris looked up; Evan had reappeared. Chris hit his forehead in frustration. His words failed him. "Quake! In Reltiv. . . !" was all he could do for an excuse.

"Did you find anyone there worth speaking to?" asked Evan wryly, knowing.

"No," admitted Chris, ashamed. He felt shaken, lost, and dependent. "I'm sorry you tried to help me and I screwed up—*again.*"

Evan touched Chris' shoulder, motioning for him to get up.

"It happens," Evan sagely pondered, as they began walking. "We want something fixed, something better, but we go about it the wrong way. We forget the Good News, that everything that matters is already taken care of." He ran the tip of his finger from one end of his cane to the other, ceremoniously.

"We get impatient with the things that don't really matter, life's little inconveniences, and think certain people will be able to help us with them, though we know from the start their motives are bad."

Chris shook his head in dejected agreement. He rubbed his neck where the backpack was chafing him.

"In fact, you'll never find anyone who won't eventually disappoint you, and your problems will never end, until you reach the Celestial City and fall into the arms of its king," said Evan.

"Where is that?" asked Christian.

"Beyond the gate, you see."

The two continued strolling. Chris asked questions he had thought about his entire life and found Evan to be a source of much wisdom. But Evan was not able to answer everything, and there seemed to be something else he wanted to say.

Suddenly, Evan stopped and looked straight into Chris's blue eyes. "There is someone I want you to see. He can give you better answers."

"Of course; just show me The Way."

* * *

Evan tapped his cane on the ground decisively. For a split second, as Chris blinked, he lost track of time and space.

Fantastically, he found himself with Evan right back at the gate, the shining gate where Evan had originally left him, only Wiseman was not there. Chris looked astonished. "How did you do that?" he asked.

"'Tis not wizardry, my boy," answered Evan. The Way to save yourself is never more than a heartbeat away. All you need to do is believe; the belief in your heart will carry you. . . "

"Knock," he further instructed. "Just knock, and you will see."

OK, thought Chris, befuddled, *but why should I knock on just a gate? I can see that we are alone and no one is behind it.*

"Things are not always as they seem, my dear lad," said Evan. "Now go ahead and do it."

Chris considered this counsel, despite being now gun-shy of advice because of Worldly Wiseman. *This man, Evan, though, is the only reason I'm still alive*, he thought.

Chris gently rapped his knuckles on the fence post, hoping for something—anything--good.

* * *

In doing so, the gate was divinely transformed into an elegant, rosewood door with intricate, symbolic carvings. Chris's second rap was met by someone already opening the door.

The door swung wide to reveal a colorful setting, totally different from the drab, brown cornfield in which Chris stood. It was a dream-like vestibule with sunny, yellow walls, an entrance into a whole new world. A gentleman with a broad smile greeted them.

"Welcome to my home here in the Christian Community of Loveland!" said the rotund, joyful man. "Please, do come in!"

With his white whiskers, rosy cheeks, sapphire eyes, and saintly demeanor, this man could be Santa Claus, Chris thought.

As Chris stepped over the door's threshold, the gentleman said, "And from this day forward you must use your full Christian name-- Christian, that is!" He delighted at the wordplay.

But how does he know my name? Christian wondered.

"And so glad to see *you*, my dear friend!" exclaimed the man, turning to Evan with cheer.

"Christian, this is Will Gooden," said Evan, by way of introduction. "Will is a loving man; I have witnessed his remarkable overtures of charity — helping anyone in want or need. He is sure to treat you most compassionately."

Gooden brushed the compliment off modestly. The exuberant, large man ushered them in through the vestibule with a long, warm swoop of the arm.

"I have always enjoyed working with this fellow," Gooden said, placing his hand on Evan's shoulder. "I have

taught him to be friendly and kind, and he has in turn
captivated many people with his important message."
Gooden directed his words toward Christian, exuding
affection and admiration. "And you, my dear boy, Evan
has told me many good things about you."

But when did Evan contact him? Christian
wondered.

Gooden offered them chairs, then got right down to
the business of helping. "What can I do for you both?"
There was no doubt that this was a most benevolent,
gracious man.

"I brought the boy here for your guidance,"
explained Evan, inspecting a ding in his cane. "Apparently,
he has been infected with hate," he said, ominously.

"I see," said Mr. Gooden, gravely.

Then Evan was gone again without notice.
Christian was disconcerted. *Why hadn't he mentioned this
hate thing earlier, and why had he left yet again?*

"Do not be distraught, my fine young lad," said Mr.
Gooden with encouragement. "Evan is near you only when
you forget The Good News. You won't see him again until
you need it. My love is enough for you now."

"Now then, allow me to get you something to eat,"
the host said, generously.

* * *

Christian ate, drank, and talked, replenishing his
body, mind, and spirit. He was comfortable in every
aspect, save one.

"Mr. Gooden," Christian pleaded, "couldn't you
possibly remove this load from my shoulders? I've been
carrying it this way for such a long time. . . since the
moment I first read my grandfather's book."

"Oh, but that burden is a good one, believe it or
not," said Mr. Gooden optimistically.

Oh no, not more lecturing on "life's little inconveniences," thought Christian. Gooden's statement annoyed and puzzled him a great deal, but the man's pure white beard gave him the look of honesty. "You see, it was at that moment that you received the Word that you finally understood what you need to know about yourself, about our true nature—about the evil core."

"But how can you be so happy--," grumbled Christian, "--so upbeat, Mr. Gooden, when you know that you, and all those around you, are every ounce bad?" He was pushing down against his backpack, grouchy.

"Because," answered Gooden with tranquility, "We still have the *choice* to decide how we will act, and that is a beautiful thing. We can fight against that contemptible nature of ours! Do not hate, Christian. Strive to do good to others at every possible turn, to love them at all cost, with no hope of anything in return."

The answer was inspiring, but the backpack he still deplored.

"Christian, I wish I could remove your burden, but you must tolerate it for the time being," said Mr. Gooden, "and bear it until you come to the place of deliverance. You will know this place when your sin does not matter anymore and is taken from you. It will be taken by someone greater than I."

"Who would or could possibly take it?" Christian asked, sad and peevish.

"Why, the King, of course, the King of this land, who lives in the Celestial City will authorize it!" answered Mr. Gooden. "He loves you more than you can imagine!" The words were flowing into Christian's whole being.

Finally, it all came together. The hate thing must have concerned his anathema toward the drug pusher, and he felt bad. Surely if the King loved him this much, he himself, Christian, could try to love the drug pusher just a little.

"I've learned a lot from today," summarized Christian, "but I have one last question. How does a person act neighborly when he has so many problems himself? It's hard to be nice when life stinks!"

But Mr. Gooden, having had a fairly easy life himself, couldn't answer.

After a time, he said, "Christian, I want you to see an acquaintance of mine. He perceives answers where no one else can see them. Then he presents certain parallels, to whisper the truth; he's gifted. I'll bring you right to him; just get on the bus."

Christian, skeptical, nevertheless followed Mr. Gooden down the avenue to the bus stop. A Greyhound soon arrived, and the boy and his guide embarked on their trip to see the man who could reportedly work miracles.

Chp. 10 "Cancel"

"For the things that are seen are temporal; but the things that are not seen are eternal." [2 Corinthians 4:18]

The charter bus flew out of town, toward another city. There, it bounced over bumpy streets, and Christian knocked into Mr. Gooden. A small, sharp charge of static zapped him, like when you rub your feet on carpet and then touch something metal. "Pardon me," Christian said, to which Mr. Gooden remarked, "It's nothing." But in that brief exchange, Christian felt as though a part of Mr. Gooden had transferred to him. He remembered not only the drug dealer but Obie and Ply as well, but no longer with ill will.

The bus stopped a few times, and each time someone got on, Will Gooden politely welcomed them, talking about the weather or noticing something nice to say.

They voyaged through tight spaces between jam-packed cars and taxis. Huge billboards and skyscrapers lined the narrow one-way streets, and the bus driver braked hard several times.

Eventually, the vehicle came to a stop in front of a decrepit, brick structure with crumbling steps, weird graffiti, and a cracked placard above the main door. "Come Ye Who are Heavy Laden," it read. Christian rose up from his seat with his backpack, Mr. Gooden in the lead. They approached the dwelling.

A slender, clean-shaven man bounded out, carrying a bag of garbage. "You bet!" he shouted behind him, with energy. He dodged around Christian and Gooden, grinning and plopping the bag into a dumpster. "Trash; filthy rags; that's the value of our works," he said quietly to himself, though good-naturedly.

"Well hello, Will! Why, I didn't recognize you!" then exclaimed the man, a youth minister who ran the place. "What brings you to our home on a beautiful day like today?" The sun was just beginning to set, and vibrant shades of orange, pink, and purple were bursting over the horizon. A shaft of light was touching the minister directly atop his head.

Will Gooden explained that Christian was in need of some "interpreting."

"My name is Pastor Interpretern, and I'll do my best to help you make sense of things," said the minister. "I'm busy, but not too busy for you. Come on in." He radiated something irresistibly reassuring, and Christian gravitated to him instantly. His personality felt like the softest, most supportive sofa you could lie on when home sick from a day of school.

He sprang up the broken steps and disappeared inside the door.

"Now I'd better be going," said Mr. Gooden. "I leave you in good hands, my dear." The boy thanked him for everything and quickly turned to follow the minister.

"Pastor, Pastor!" Christian heard as he cautiously entered the shelter. A girl was calling for him to come look at her homework. "Just a minute, Cindy," Interpretern answered. "Christian," he called, "come on in and meet my bunch."

In a large living area where several teens were clustered, some sprawled out on the floor doing their school work, some cozily nestled on couches conversing, Christian met the reasons the minister lived. Christian sat down on a chair, backpack still obviously nagging.

*   *   *

Interpretern had picked up on something in the boy already and had an idea. "The two not here," he added, "are in their rooms. They're little, and they're just waking up from their nap. But you might as well meet them right now."

He showed Christian down a wing and into the room of two very young girls. "Christian, this is Passion and Patience," he said, pointing to two diminutive preschool children. "Passion and Patience have been inseparable since they came to the shelter."

What he said next he said off to the side, so as the children would not hear. "When they were first brought here, separately, of course, Passion had such a temper. 'Now! Now! Now!' she would holler. Her tantrums, and messes. . ."

"After a few days," he explained, "she developed a sky-high fever. The fever was like a fire raging inside her, and, after time in the hospital with no improvement, we feared she was dying." The minister was pushing back tears.

"But then Patience came," he went on. "She looked just like little Passion! But she was so quiet and reserved, never making a fuss. One of the kids got the bright idea to bring Patience to see Passion, in the hopes that maybe having a new friend her age might just bring her back from the brink."

"Patience sat at Passion's bedside. 'Please don't go just yet,' she begged Passion, 'you have to be patient.' She prayed steadily and cried often--cried so many tears that it was like a little brook spilling down from Heaven. The prayers cancelled the effects of the illness, and Passion got better right away!"

"Well, since Patience came," he finished, "Passion settled right down. It was uncanny, really. Patience has a way of soothing her." The minister lifted the corners of his mouth into a satisfied smile. "Yes, Passion has learned a lot from that little girl."

"They're cute kids," remarked Christian, watching them on the carpeted floor, coloring groggily. Passion was drawing a picture of red and orange flames, while Patience was drawing a picture of a waterfall. They shared the crayons in seamless exchanges, and harmony reigned in their little abode.

The boy and the minister quietly closed the door on the children till it remained open to just a crack.

"What I really think happened to cause that illness," said Interpretern, as though he were revealing something deep, "is that Passion had wanted to go see the King before her time. (You know how little kids are—everything seems like an eternity.) I'm sure so did Patience, but she knew she had to wait."

"The king of the Celestial City?" asked Christian.

"That's right," said the minister. "You'll meet him too someday if you continue your journey."

"But what about *now*?!" asked Christian, identifying with Passion's desire, her flames and her fire. "Can't I meet him now?!"

"He lives so very far away. If you really wished, you could try and harm yourself, and you'd be there right now, but know that He wouldn't meet you. That's why you must remember Patience and make the full journey, no matter how hard it gets."

Christian thought back to the moment of his grandfather's death when he had wanted to give up and leave the world with him; he also remembered the recent scene at the Slew where he hadn't put up quite the heroic fight.

* * *

The minister ushered Christian out the front door, picking up on something else. "There's an outside and an inside to every person's situation," said Interpretern to the boy. "Won't you tell me about yours?"

Christian began to open up to the minister as they went, telling him about his home life: his parents' divorce and grandfather's death, his ongoing poverty and embarrassments at school. "I'm not popular or smart," he confessed.

The minister replied, "But you are real."

This wasn't much consolation; it only reminded him of an empty fairy tale he had read as a boy.

Soon afterwards, they were traveling in the fragrant evening air out to the affluent district. "Houses are like people," Interpretern said, mysteriously. "I'm going to show you some things, to give you perspective."

They came to a rising, semicircular driveway bordered by two long curves of imported, ornamental trees. At the top of the arch was a well-lit mansion, a gigantic residence elevated up from the earth like a palace. Freshly painted in gleaming alabaster, with crystal windows, its splendor made Christian' eyes dilate.

There was a six-car garage with paneled, bronze doors, two of which were opened to reveal a red sports car and silver limo. A woman clad in glamorous, silk brocade and diamonds stepped into the Rolls-Royce, and it sped away.

"What an awesome house!" shouted Christian, animated, although Interpretern frowned.

Christian could hardly wait to go in.

Chp. 11 **"Left Behind"**

"In thy life thou receivedst thy good things, and likewise Lazarus evil things: but now he is comforted, and thou art tormented."
[Luke 16:25]

There was a long line of people waiting to go into the mansion. Strangely, though, Pastor Interpretern passed through them, as if he were invisible. He motioned for Christian to come.

Interpretern pushed the spectacular front door open and walked right in, without even ringing the bell. "It's all right, Christian; trust me," he said.

They advanced through a gorgeous, opulent reception area, filled with sparkling glass chandeliers, red velvet furniture, and an impressive spiral staircase. They moved onward, into a lavish drawing room like a museum, filled with ivory statues of modern-day wealthy and prestigious people on marble pedestals.

"Now we'll see the parts they actually live in," the minister told his young protégé. Christian was perplexed.

Beyond the stunning entranceway and drawing
room lay a dark chamber. They entered there, and the door
slammed shut behind them.

This room was nothing like the others. An ominous
vibe; an ugly secret; an appalling scene greeted them. . . A
man was pent up in a ridiculously small, iron cage. His
minute, oppressive enclosure left no room for him to even
stand. Disheveled, greasy hair framed his pale face, and a
dirty cloth around his gaunt hips accentuated a protruding
rib cage. He was moaning something inscrutable, as if
complaining to the air.

"First, you demean yourself for not being popular,
Christian, for not having money. . .," said Interpretern. "But
this man was formerly what you apparently aspire to. Oh,
he had plenty of funds and friends all right! His pretend
pals were there to help it all happen: gambling, drinking,
carousing, you name it, he did it. So much so that all his
little pursuits became his undoing. Money and charm wear
thin, you know."

Wanting to show empathy, Christian decided to talk
to the man. "I'm sorry about your friends—I don't have
real friends e--"

The wraith of a man only snarled and spat back, like
a rabid dog.

"Not very charming now, is he?" remarked the
minister, rhetorically. "Sorry, but you can't talk to him.
Not even the magic of goodwill you brought with you is
likely to work at this point. Unfortunately, he has an
irreparable, hardened heart. He's shut off from you, he's
shut off from me, and he's shut off from the King," said
Interpretern, full of remorse. "He prefers his containment
to going back out into the World for more, I suppose."

Christian, dumbfounded, followed his guide out of
the man's quarters.

"Second, you demean yourself by saying you're
such a poor student, but just look through there," said the

minister, pointing to a tiny peep hole in a solid wall of books. Stacks upon stacks of outdated volumes fit tightly to the ceiling, and the sight inside was disturbing. The lone occupant was pacing to and fro, stirring up clouds of dust between musty, old tomes. He was smashing into tables and sending glass vials crashing to the floor all around him. Shards crunched beneath his bare feet, though he went on in the dim light as if he didn't care. His paper fortress was impenetrable to even Christian's hardest thrust.

"Oh, don't bother trying to knock his walls down now," said Interpretern. "He was a brilliant academician, a daring scholar, a well-respected and accomplished professor, known the world over; he possessed titles and accolades like you wouldn't believe. Every day he received answers from test tubes and instruments, experiments and equations. But he couldn't allow himself to believe in what might lie beyond the data perceived with our senses, the information beyond his four walls; he couldn't make the leap of faith that you, a mere boy, has made. Again, he's been left behind, I'm afraid."

"Surely that man--he's being held against his will?" queried Christian.

"No, he is not. Like the other, he has *chosen* to be here. If you asked him, he'd just tell you to leave him alone," said Interpretern.

As Christian looked again through the tiny hole, he saw the man suddenly kneel on the floor, and wildly throw his arms in the air, not in despair, but as if in praise.

"He's made his own intelligence and knowledge into his god," explained Interpretern, "and he certainly doesn't want any interference from us. He's quite at home here, I assure you."

"So what are you saying? That they'll be left here alone forever?" asked Christian.

"I'm saying that you need to keep inside the *right* walls—the walls of the pathway to the King. You'll know them. They'll be high and thick at first, for discipline. They will mark The Way; they will keep you headed in the best direction. But they'll be two, not four-- and certainly not barred-- to keep you open to living. As for the death and divorce you're dealing with, allow me to show you the next room."

"Oh please, let's go," said Christian to his guide. "I don't like this place. It looks so good on the outside, but when you get inside. . ."

"Of course," said the minister. "We'll leave right away." The two stepped out into the night.

They were by now back on the lawn, and Christian, being hungry, reached up to a tree to pick a piece of fruit. But of course there was none there.

"I've got to return to the orphanage; there might be a delivery of food tonight," said Pastor Interpretern. "Are you all set to go on your own?"

"Sure," said Christian, faking courage.

He turned to take in the sight of the impressive mansion once more. This time, however, he noticed something he had not spotted before. He could see people, maybe hundreds, swarming like flies, walking on the flat roof of the estate. Leading to it was the long line of people he had seen upon first arriving. They formed a snake-like coil that wound around the side of the house and up a fire escape.

Christian inquired, "Before you go, can you tell me why all those people are up there?"

"Yes," said his interpreter. "I know fully why. Those people are waiting to get in to live here. They want to experience the luxury, the lifestyle, the fame. The owner gives them tickets, some with 'winning' numbers on them, and they wait and they wait and they wait."

"Until they die?" asked Christian.

"Well, you've seen what happens to the 'lucky' ones, but the rest, yes, they wait. . . until they die."

"So how were we able to just waltz right in there, ahead of the line, if everyone's supposed to wait?" asked Christian, nonplussed.

"You and I, Christian, we were just passing through. We're hopefully headed somewhere better. Best of luck in getting there."

And with that, Interpretern waved and walked away, leaving Christian to fend for himself.

Chp. 12 **"Him"**
"Thy sins be forgiven." [Mark 2:5]

Christian mulled over the ghastly images that he had witnessed in the mansion, and he was terrified. But in the velvet darkness of the evening, he resolved to carry on, to try to find the road with the high walls that Interpretern had told him to look for.

Christian plodded wearily away. He walked on for hours, hoping that he would be able to find a regular house with lights on. But it occurred to him that he was out in a rural, unpopulated area.

Sometime before midnight, Christian saw those high, thick cement walls. They marked a steep ascent up a dangerous highway. The pavement was uneven and cracked. Tackling this part of the journey was going to be difficult, especially still burdened under the backpack.

His steps up the incline were tedious. The more the angle increased, the less his legs served him. His calf muscles burned; his knee joints buckled. His energy was dissipating though his heart was pounding hard.

Christian would frequently stumble or slip, uncoordinated from extreme fatigue. Unbeknownst to him, a strap had become dislodged and his Bible had fallen from his pack. Once when he faltered, his palm came down hard on a sharp rock. He screamed like a barbarian to process the pain.

He was perspiring profusely, and his clothes were now drenched with sweat. He felt more uncomfortable in this dirty, smelly, old outfit than at any other time in his life. His cheap, old sneakers rubbed his ankles raw. *Blisters are forming, no doubt.*

An occasional car would pass, speeding by with no concern. In his mind, the cars were there to antagonize him, emphasizing the fact that he was slow and incapable. Each time one flew by, because the roadway was so narrow, he had to jump to avoid it, and press himself tightly against the wall. The wall's gravel poked his chest through his shirt.

He began to curse as he went. With every heave of his backpack, he convinced himself that the hill was insurmountable. *What's the use?!!* Christian cried. *No one could conquer this hill!*

Christian picked apart the logic of an absentee king who would ask his subjects to perform the impossible without any help. *If the King could see me, I'd look like a tiny ant to Him, or an almost invisible speck--a grain of sand in the Sahara Desert.*

His backpack was insufferable. It loaded him down with bad memories. He realized he had no other option than to put up with this "inconvenience," as Evan and Gooden had spoken of, for the rest of his life. *But what had Grandpa said about the Bible and its power to help?* Christian desperately longed for the opportunity to stop and search for the answer.

Just as he thought that, he noticed the slope had changed. He was on flat land, a plateau of some sort. *Finally! An even plane!* He took a deep breath and reached around to the side pocket of the backpack where the Bible had been, but before he could even discover it was missing, he saw something.

Right there in the roadway was a tall cross. About eight feet high, it was a white, wooden cross, with pink and blue artificial flowers tied to it. There was a weathered, tan teddy bear, and a small, melancholy sign on which some poor child's death had been memorialized. It dawned on Christian that he was standing at a past crash site, undoubtedly the scene of horrendous anguish, unspeakable woe.

Christian studied the cross for a long time. There was a break in the concrete wall behind it, about the width of a coffin. Christian glanced into the dim void, but all he could see was the steepest descent imaginable, surely not a better way to go.

The silk roses were beautiful, the teddy bear soft, the cross rugged. *How ironic they can't help anyone now.*

*   *   *

Suddenly, the stuffed animal and flowers were gone, in their place a clear-white human body, the ghostlike shape of a man. It was clinging to the cross, held up by three crudely fashioned, nine-inch nails. A supernatural flow of blood was dripping from the piercings. Otherworldly, faint blue beams of light radiated out from the body.

What Christian was seeing was so incredible that he thought he must be hallucinating. He shook his head in an effort to clear his brain. Still, the translucent entity hung on the cross. It made no motion. It was the semblance of a man who was obviously dead.

Christian dropped to his knees, screaming straight up into the sky. "Why did you take them, God! Why the boy, your beloved child? Why this man, your very own Son?"

The mysterious blue rays around the corpse intensified.

The weight of Christian's pack was cutting into his shoulders, enough to tear flesh. "You never cared about us down here! You never cared!" he shrieked in torment.

It was at that instant that Christian's pack miraculously just fell away from him. The shadow of an arm grasped the pack and rolled the unbearable load. Christian, frozen, watched as the bag that had caused so much misery simply tumbled into the dark abyss.

It's gone, he heard, telepathically. *Into the mouth of The Grave. . . Your sins are forgiven.*

Then, audibly came the same voice saying, "He did it for you; He did it for us all!" Christian looked up to the sweet sight of Evan standing there, gesturing to the figure fastened unnaturally to the cross. "Jesus," Evan said. With an exhilarating feeling of lightness and the ecstasy of complete relief, Christian soaked in the overwhelming sensation of deepest peace.

* * *

Christian had been bowing his head in awe and reverence for some time. When he looked up, Evan's visitation was over, fleeting as usual. And the flowers and teddy bear had resumed their place on the cross, the vision of Jesus now gone.

Christian looked to see how high the rest of the hill would be. *Not far*, he said to himself.

He progressed up the short remainder. Climbing was so much easier without the backpack's weight! When he reached the apex, he paused for a moment to take in the view. It was hard to see much, being that it was night, but he could see a few clumps of lights in the distance, probably villages. Christian stood up straight and tall, thanking God for removing his cumbersome burden and having helped him vanquish the monstrous hill.

Suddenly, three glowing forms appeared before him. Clad in long, simple white robes, they approached Christian with outpourings of congratulations. "My beloved child," spoke one. "With you He is well pleased. Let us anoint you." He waved his hands over the boy and, as he did that, a much-needed change of apparel appeared. The loose-fitting, caped garment was made of the softest white satin imaginable, and it magically replaced his foul-smelling, blood-and-mud-smeared clothes. Christian felt like a newborn baby, so pure and innocent, fresh.

The second spirit bestowed upon Christian a most eloquent blessing. He said that because Christian was so adored by the King, he would be monitored and protected by leagues of angels. He reached out to Christian's forehead, and, with two gentle, loving strokes, drew a small, black cross from ashes.

The third spirit gave him a certificate, an antique scroll tied up with red ribbon. "Take care to preserve this," he instructed. "You will have to present it at your final destination."

Christian, being eager to know what it said, asked if he could open it.

"Yes," was all that was said.

Trembling, Christian carefully unrolled it. The following was printed at the top: "The bearer of this paper receives admittance into the Celestial City." Then, he saw his name at the bottom, in the most beautiful, refined silver script.

Part 2: The Demons

Chapter 13: "Check-outs and Short-Cuts"

"Go to the ant, thou sluggard; consider her ways, and be wise."
[Proverbs 6:6]

A bittersweet moment seized Christian. His jubilation over the angels' promises, mixed with regret for his mistakes, carried Christian away as he read his name on the certificate. *I've done nothing to deserve this,* he thought. *Nothing. I even screamed, rejected Him,* he pondered with a shudder, then paused. *It is only through the grace of God. . .* he could hear another of his grandfather's old sayings.

He would believe in Jesus, he *surely* would believe, he promised himself, as well as Evan and the King, in his heart. In his satin raiment, he felt different, he looked different, and he would certainly act different (better) in the future, as best as he very well could. He was recharged and ready to go face the world a changed boy. He rerolled the note carefully and put it in a pocket next to his heart.

It was sometime in the wee hours of the morning. The hill began its smooth descent, the roadway still flanked by high walls. Christian easily made his way down, moving much faster than he had going up. Having no burden on his back, his steps were buoyant and airy.

* * *

At the base of the hill, in a shallow ditch against one wall, he found three teenagers asleep, snoring loudly. They looked dirty and unkempt and had chains and monitors around their bare ankles, all three of them linked together.

Christian gently nudged them, but they did not awake. The spot where they lay was dangerous, and a slight wind was beginning to whip, so Christian thought it important to get them to move.

After much prodding, one, and then another eventually woke, but not the third.

"Hi," said Christian, bending low. "My name's Christian, . . .want some help? Not many people are out at three o'clock in the morning! Please, tell me your names."

"Uh, Sim," said one, slowly, in a bovine tone.

"And my name's Manny," said the other, more intelligibly.

"Thank you for telling me," said Christian. "Now, how can I help you take these chains off? I know what it's like to be weighed down."

"Uh," said Sim, drowsily, "no."

"We're fine hanging out here together. We're all friends," said Manny, backing Sim's quick refusal, only with more words.

Christian was a little shocked, although he wanted to respect the teens' feelings. He proceeded slowly, ultimately hoping to get to the root of the problem. "Tell me," he said with concern, "how did you get this way—the chains I mean?"

"Well, to tell ya the truth," Manny confided in Christian, "we put them on ourselves, so to speak. Then we put them together; what I mean is, we all met up in detox and hit it right off. "

"O.K., but why are you all out here in a place like this?" asked Christian.

"Well, yesterday, we were being transported from one facility to another, and we managed to escape." The girl, Manny, responded with a certain strange flatness, an absence of some necessary human spark. "Now, we're just waitin' to make our next move. But don't worry, man, we're not gonna use again or anything like that--we just gotta regroup. So don't report us, OK?"

Christian saw an empty medicine bottle, lid off, some stray pills on the ground near sleeping Seth.

"I've got some news that is going to be great for you. It's going to help you start fresh," said Christian with tearful enthusiasm. "There's a place you can go to where you'll never need drugs again."

"Not another detox," moaned Sim.

"All of us been through at least five so far," Manny explained, "and they're all the same. Sometimes you get better, but usually not."

"No, that's not what I'm talking about," answered Christian. "Where I'm talking about, there's a love better than any high you could ever get with drugs. Come with me, and you will live forever in happiness!" Christian urged.

"No," returned Sim, bluntly. "We'd just want to check out after a day or so, same as before."

"But this place I'm talking about is different. Would you like to talk about it?" asked Christian.

"No, don't bother," replied Sim. "We don't care about 'forever.' We're just trying to get through today."

"But you've got to think of tomorrow!" exclaimed Christian. "Manny," he said, addressing the other poor, misguided soul, "do you agree with your friend?"

"Ya, I agree with him," she responded, without really thinking.

"But wouldn't you like to at least hear about how I know such a place exists?"

"Listen, buddy," replied Manny, "I know what I know, and that's what's most important. . . Everybody knows what they need to know from their very own mind-- already," she said.

"Do you really believe that the answers to the secrets of life are inside ourselves?" asked Christian.

"Maybe not inside *Sim*," she joked aside to her witless partner, "or this one here." She was pointing to Seth. "He's just too lazy to think." Seth went on sleeping fitfully, rolling over in visible distress, as if possessed by some kind of continuous nightmare.

The King in his kingdom shed three tears then. One was for simple Sim, who never bothered about anything. (*Did he still take drugs because there was nothing better to do out there, or was it that the drugs had numbed him to change?*) The second was for slothful Seth, who would "check out" on life, burying his hurts and questions in drugs, instead of expending the energy required to confront them head-on. The last tear was for the presumptuous Manny Presuntion, who, having grown up with drugs all around her, had never thought far enough outside "the box" of her own little self-absorbed mind to be open to the possibility of a different life. The three tears froze into sleet as they were coming down from the sky.

Christian felt the first pieces of cold, sharp drizzle fall down from above, as Manny and Sim retreated into their little hole. Christian told himself to mentally "shake the dust off his feet" as Jesus had said when people wouldn't listen. Christian walked away grimly, considering the misfortune of these three uninspired souls.

* * *

All of a sudden, Christian caught sight of two older men walking along the level highway in the same direction as he was. They were proceeding painfully slowly, being quite elderly. As Christian overtook them, one turned and smiled.

"Hello, I'm Mr. Heipokracy," he said, "but you can call me 'Hip.'"

" I'm Mr. Formalist," said the other, tersely.

"Hi, I'm Christian," said the boy. The travelers' clean clothes, glasses, and polite manners were signs of potential intellect and decency. "I am surprised to meet people this early in the morning on such a remote highway as this. . . We've probably got a storm coming," he said, trying to be friendly.

"We're on our way to the Celestial City," said Mr. Formalist, dryly.

"How did you do making it over that brutal hill?" Christian asked, interested to know how they could have had enough stamina.

"Oh," snickered Mr. Heipokracy, "we didn't go over the hill, silly boy!"

"Well, then, how did you get here? There's no other roads that I can see anywhere," observed Christian, suspicious.

"We took a short-cut," said Hip proudly, as if he had had the smartest idea since sliced bread. "You know, you didn't *have* to go over that beastly hill. Not many people I know do. It's hard, far too hard. Better to think smart, not hard."

Mr. Formalist went on, as if trying to do a better job of explaining. "We came from a very big tourist district that's just the other side of this wall, you see. It's teeming with people who come over just like we did."

"As a matter of fact, it's all set up! You just get on a special escalator. Thank goodness for modern conveniences, eh?" Hip nudged Mr. Formalist with his elbow and smiled on one side of his mouth.

Mr. Formalist was not amused.

Christian felt as though something wasn't right. He thought back to Evan, to Mr. Gooden, to Pastor Interpretern. They had never mentioned an alternate route.

"You know, Christian, I've always been a Christian," continued Mr. Heipokracy, talking in circles, sounding somewhat cocky, "and I'm a real good one. I go to church every Sunday—sit right up in the front row every time. I give 'em loads of money, too! OK, so I haven't always been exactly a 'saint' outside of church, but I'm basically good, I'd have to say. I know we'll be to the Celestial City within days, and the Country Club there will be glad to have us! We'll soon be enjoying all it has to offer."

"Oh, you old fool," blurted the cantankerous Mr. Formalist, miserably. "They'll never let you in! You're not on par, and you didn't really earn it."

There was bravado in his voice as he addressed Christian next. "I, on the other hand, have been irrefutably spotless and have gone above and beyond the call of duty! I've tried to get Hip here to practice his golf swings and buy the right clothes so he'd be sure to get accepted, but he doesn't listen."

He then spoke to Hip again. "You should have at least gone through the motions! I always pray ninety-five prayers a day, one for every putt! The King appreciates numbers, you know."

Christian realized that these men had already heard the Good News, but it had dried up within them long ago. *They're set in their ways,* Christian heard telepathically, and he knew the voice all right—Evan's.

They felt the sting of the sleet coming faster now. The two old gentlemen raised their black umbrellas. Just then, a slow-moving hearse passed them, and turned about a mile ahead onto the first cross-street. It was a short street, marked with a sign that read "Dead End."

Chp. 14 **"Push"**
"Oh wretched man that I am." [Romans 7:24]

The angry storm was full-blown now, some time

after Christian had passed the two old men. The sleet pummeled him. Unfortunately, Christian could see another hill in the distance that he would soon have to tackle. *Push,* he said to himself.

The hill didn't look near as bad as the first, although the inclement weather was a force to be reckoned with. A grayish-green gargoyle sat at the base, its stone mouth smiling, as if to wish him luck.

Christian began to climb, despite the biting, driving sleet. His certificate was still safely in his pocket. He wanted to take it out and reread it, but he knew it would get ruined. *Push,* he said to himself.

Not far into the climb, Christian heard a noise-- someone yelling, though the content was indistinguishable.

"Noooooooo!" came a person's voice through the raging wind.

Then another, sounding like: "Keep going, keep goin'!"

A girl and a boy were running full speed, straight toward him. Their legs could barely keep up with the downward slant. Their arms were circling like windmills gone crazy. They ran right by Christian, one on either side of him, hardly noticing.

"Hey!" shouted Christian. He hoped they would stop.

They didn't slow down for anything, but when they got to the bottom of the hill, the boy glanced back, hand raised to his brow to see and shield himself from the sleet.

"Don't go up that hill!" the boy yelled as loudly as he could, to penetrate the gale. "There's something terrible up there!"

Christian quickly ran back down so as to hear them better, to get details. The gargoyle was frowning now, or so Christian thought, though he didn't have time to re-check it. He whipped out the full width of his cape and attempted to shield the two travelers.

Under the white tarp, huddled on the ground close together, the two boys shook till their body heat gradually warmed them. The girl sat as far away as possible.

The boy told Christian his name, Tim Morris, and the girl's (Missy Strust), though she protested. They had been journeying to the Celestial City, but had emphatically decided to turn back.

Christian asked what that "something terrible" was. *Was it a demon? A monster?*

Oh no; there was a lion up there!

"Its fangs were this long!" cried Tim, gesturing hysterically with his outspread arms.

"There's no way I'd have gone up there if I knew what was in store for me! I should never have trusted my preacher's directions!" whined Missy.

Tim nodded his head in agreement and began blubbering excessively. Missy looked askance at Christian, wondering if she should even be there with him now. While these two teenagers wallowed in their fitful reactions, Christian decided to stop and think. "Let's pray," he suggested.

In moments, the sky cleared a bit. It was just before dawn, and the sun wanted to blink over the horizon.

Christian drew back his cloak and all three stood up. Sullen looks were all that Missy and Tim could accomplish.

Christian felt drained.

*   *   *

Suddenly, Christian saw two black umbrellas bobbing along the edge of the road. As they approached, Christian could see that they were the old men catching up. Christian took the young people aside, quickly. "Please, don't tell them about what you've seen at the top, how afraid you were. They may be able to do what you couldn't. . . "

The five travelers greeted one another. Tim and Missy complied and said nothing about what awaited.

The group then decided to part. Tim and Missy retreated; Formalist and Hip continued on with Christian. *Push,* Christian said to himself.

It wasn't long before the two old men were complaining of the exertion up the hill, bemoaning their situation, and bickering with one another.

"I thought you said there wasn't supposed to be anything harder than a mild stroll?!" quavered Formalist to his companion.

"Can't you see the road coming up that cuts across and goes to either side?" demanded Hip feebly.

"Yes, of course, but I also see ropes there, Hip."

"But I've got snippers, Formalist. We'll be able to get around the hard part without even trying!" Hip pat his pocket. "And nobody'll be the wiser," he reassured his comrade.

So when the three travelers reached the intersection halfway up, Mr. Heipokracy cut the rope barricade. Christian watched as the men stood and argued about which way to go, left or right. Their disagreement grew heated, until at last they decided to go their separate ways.

"So that's the thanks I get, after forty-eight years!" rattled Formalist, nastily.

"Aw, stuff it in your ear, old man!" shouted back Hip. Christian watched them plod away in opposite directions, until his eyes could follow them no more around the bends.

* * *

Christian had to push through his worry about the lion and get to the top. *Better to face the fear straight on.*

Sheer adrenaline kept Christian going. He marched onward, determined to see this lion. He saw nothing but cement walls for the longest time. Finally, he was able to see a stately, pink structure in the distance.

The road abruptly ended, and a graceful yet steep stone path without walls picked it up. Christian soon saw a watch dog, not a lion, standing sentinel. The dog was growling viciously, and its fangs were, to be sure, very long. However, it was chained to a stone pillar, and only doing its job.

So, with no further ado, Christian calmly, assertively passed the dog through the gate of the yard. Although the dog alerted to his scent, the white light of Christian's clothes pacified it, and it stopped snarling. In fact, it cocked its head curiously and then whimpered, as if begging for affection. Christian went to it and stroked its head. It rubbed against his leg. *Tim, what a timorous coward,* thought Christian, *and Missy, what a mistrustful mistake.*

With the dog no longer a threat, Christian continued up the path's gentle rise. He had arrived successfully at the top of this second difficult hill. Christian remembered the angels at the top of the first. He was sure that the marking on his forehead had washed off, but he still had his certificate and hoped it was dry. He reached into his left breast pocket to touch it, his soul craving to replay its powerful words. But the pocket was empty. . .

Chp. 15 "Give Us This Day Our Daily Bread"

"But now I desire a better country, that is, an heavenly." *[Hebrews 11:15-16]*

Christian was in a terrible panic because he had lost his certificate. He double-checked his pocket, but nothing. Rapidly, he rehearsed his steps to try to pinpoint when it could have fallen out. The last time he remembered having it was just before he met Tim and Missy at the base of the hill. He decided to turn back and carefully scour the terrain until he found it.

If only I had been more responsible,. . . he said to himself with inward humiliation at not having guarded it better. He prayed for God to help. Christian kept looking, his eyes scanning side to side fruitlessly in the darkness for the priceless certificate. Old, familiar put-downs flooded his mind as if to say, *See, you really are a loser. Try as you might, you can't keep anything good. Just like your father.*

When Christian arrived at the bottom of the hill, again, he saw the spot at which he and Tim and Missy had sat under his cloak, waiting the storm out. The gargoyle had an uncertain, quizzical look on its face this time. The first rays of dawn were now streaming over the horizon, and Christian wondered how he had marshaled enough energy not to have slept for a whole night.

Just beyond that spot, there was a sewer grate with something stuck in it, something white flapping in the breeze. Christian ran to it, picked it up, and confirmed it as his treasure. He was ecstatic to have it back! He inspected it for damage; there was none except a slight tear. He carefully placed it back in his pocket and breathed a sigh of relief.

I've found it! I've found it! What are the odds of that?! But then he said, inside where recriminations waited, *I've wasted so much time. . . Why was I so stupid? Why didn't I check it more often?* He began his third climb up the same hill, still dejected.

And if that weren't bad enough, he now realized that his Bible was missing; he assumed it had gone down with the backpack into the mouth of the abyss.

* * *

When Christian got to the crossroad again that

morning, where Hip and Formalist had strayed, he peered down it both ways and saw several people, though none of them were the old men. So he went on and made it back up the steep stone path, though more lethargically than he had the first time, and the dog was a welcomed sight now. He let it smell his hand, and the animal remembered that they were friends.

Christian again could make out that pinkish-colored place, the morning sun shining behind it. It was an old church swathed in plaster, claiming the top of the hill. Its architecture had a Spanish flair, and the marquee outside the arched doors read "House of the Holy." A man was standing out in front, waving a handful of tracts.

"Mee name ees Watch Portare," he said, smiling. He said that it was his job to watch for pilgrims, and then help them in through the church door. He beckoned Christian in, placing his hand on Christian's back, escorting him proudly.

The sanctuary possessed great beauty. Christian's eyes rose in awe up to the magnificent vaulted ceiling, with paintings that looked like Michelangelo himself had done them. There were stained-glass windows at intervals along the side of the royal blue interior, and an altar displaying precious relics. An immense, ruby-studded chalice rested on a dazzling cloth of purple and gold. Incense burned in the front, and a thousand candles glowed in tiny, scarlet glass cups.

The man, Watch Porter, kindly said, "Seet down ond rayst, mee neenyo." The two sat in a pew near the back. It was pleasantly warm in the church, and Christian felt at ease. He began to grow sleepy.

The man roused him.

"Sorry," said Christian. "I've been walking all through the night from my town far away. I'm looking for the Celes, Celes,. . ." He was slurring his speech, he was that tired.

"Layt me breeng ju to thay priest's rooms to slayp," the man suggested.

Christian got up and followed him.

"We'll hayve toe talk weeth hees daughtares, though, baycoose thay priest ees attayndeeng dos muertes." The man suddenly realized he had slipped back into Spanish and quickly translated the last phrase as "two deaths."

Watch Porter told Christian that the priest was very, very busy with some people who had just an hour ago brought two bodies to the church. The victims were old men who had died in freak accidents.

"One pawsed by falleeng eento a peet and breakeeng hees heep," explained Watch Porter. "Thee othare, he pawsed by being hod by oneemals."

Oh no, thought Christian, realizing what had happened. *Poor old Heipokracy and Formalist! It must have been them. I knew they shouldn't have gone off the main path.* Christian shuddered as he pictured one being torn to ribbons by feral animals (it had been Formalist) and the other calling out in pain from broken bones, a fractured hip, bleeding to death from internal injuries (that had been Hip).

Watch Porter helped Christian through the church, down several halls, and into the attached rectory. There, a vibrant, pretty girl named Discrecion, one of the nuns, rushed to see what was the commotion.

"Oh, my," she said, sweetly though alarmed. Immediately, her fair sisters, Prudence, Piety, and Charity, ran out to see as well. As Porter helped to lift Christian onto a spare bed, the four teenage girls eagerly gathered around him and launched a flurry of questions. "What is your name? Where did you come from? Why those clothes?" They barraged him, their curiosity insatiable.

For a full hour or more, they engrossed themselves in Christian's account of his journey thus far. He told them about leaving home, being rescued from quicksand, and escaping from the quake. He mentioned knocking at the gate, and going with Mr. Gooden and Interpretern. He described his visions of Jesus and the angels and narrated his run-ins with the chained kids and the old men. His audience listened attentively, often inserting gasps or "oohs" and "ahs." He delighted in showing them how he pet the dog despite the others' warnings, and that was the last that Christian could remember before sleep enveloped him. . .

* * *

As Christian slept, Rodney woke. It was almost 2 AM, or so the clock on the jail wall indicated. He sat straight up in bed. *God, what a dream!* He was glad he hadn't screamed and woken up all his cellmates. Or had he been moaning in his sleep? *I've got to look tough to them, or I'll never make it here.* He had absolutely no idea why he was having this dream, or what it all meant, but he was a little afraid now, afraid to go back to sleep, afraid to even be. He lay back down, pulling the ratty blanket binding closely around his head. The numbers on the clock were glowing an eerie green. He watched the second hand make its revolutions, the minute hand move slowly, silently, between the eleven and twelve. After thirteen minutes, he was asleep again, and right back into the same dream.

* * *

It was early morning of the following day. Christian had slept all through the day he had arrived; that is what Porter was saying. Christian was in a comfortable bed, covered with a thick, handmade quilt, and surrounded by the five amiable faces of his new friends. The first thing he did was check his pocket, and luckily, his certificate was still there. *I want to stay here forever,* he said to himself, peacefully.

"Well, up and Adam! You can't stay in this bed forever," urged the sweet Discrecion. "We have been waiting for you for breakfast!" She took his hand. "Mama has made you some delicious bread este manana, and the Good Lord will use it to give you strength."

Christian could hear his grandfather's voice saying, "Give us this day our daily bread." Here, at least, he felt that all was right with the world.

Chp. 16 "God's Arms"
"He had fought with and slain him that had the power of death." [Hebrews 2:14]

Christian, Watch Porter, Discrecion, and her sisters sat down to a delicious feast. Christian looked at Discrecion, who was so beautiful with her dark eyes and long eyelashes. He couldn't help but staring.

When they were finished, his hosts wanted to show him some things they felt were "very important." Watch Porter took him to a room that looked like a library of infinite space, and there, among all kinds of artifacts inside special cases, Watch began to pull out files of historical records. Every good deed of all time was preserved in old-fashioned writing here, no matter how miniscule or unseen by the world. In particular, there was an antique-looking master list many feet long of soldiers and veterans, names of people who had ever served Christ as his warriors.

Pointing to that list, Porter said, "Mee nino, eet ees my weesh that jur name appayer hare un dia." Christian wasn't sure what he meant exactly, or how his name could possibly find its way there, but he listened eagerly for Watch's next words anyway.

Next, the nuns and Watch ushered Christian into an armory containing an impressive collection of weapons, some ancient, some modern, but all to be used for good. There were knives, spears, swords, and guns; armor, helmets, shields, and bullet-proof vests. There were also the most famous armaments used in the Bible: Gideon's trumpets and lamps, Samson's jaw-bone club, David's sling and stone. All of them, and more, were there. Porter said, "Et ees my weesh that jou gate some protaktion."

Porter showed Christian a full-length mirror. "Look," he said, standing slightly behind, "Ju are ah mahn ofe Gode, boot ju are combeeng eento hosteel terreetory."

Porter handed him some gear, and Christian put on his new equipment over his white satin raiment.

"There are mawny people who have haylped ju along thay way so far. Now ju weel hawve a chance to haylp othares." Help others: it was a tall order. But Watch talked to Christian, and Christian, encouraged, resolved to enter the World again with greater authority. He patted his special letter from the King now safely inside his new protective suit.

"Thank you,—for everything," said Christian.

"No, thank *you*, my dearest warrior," said Discrecion when she saw the handsome Christian outfitted for battle.

"What for?" Christian asked.

"For doing God's work," she replied, standing there so captivatingly, the embodiment of purity and innocence that Christian longed for.

Then Christian looked around. Charity, Piety, Prudence, and Porter: he knew he had to do it for them as well. He promised he would be brave.

Christian and Discrecion glanced shyly at one another for a few more moments, lingering and not wanting to part. But then Christian walked away.

"Vaya con Dios," Porter and the girls shouted, waving their arms in the air, smiling and crying.

Chp. 17 **"Going Down"**
"He had gone but a little way before he espied a foul fiend coming over the field to meet him." [Revelation 9:11]

So it was in this way that Christian, on the afternoon of the third day of his adventure, left the House of the Holy and his new friends, somewhat sadly, though with a very big sense of purpose. *Maybe it might even be fun to do some fighting!* he daydreamed.

He picked up the road again. The hill's downward gradient was mild. The valley he was coming into was pleasant. Little did he know, he was walking into the Valley of Humiliation, where a terrible, hideous monster was lying in wait for those on the road to the Celestial City.

Dusk was coming on quickly. Christian marched on unwittingly through the countryside. The road, now a path, was less defined here. The chilly autumnal valley grew dimmer. The trees were gnarled, some rotting. There were objects hanging on some of their branches, like a crown of thorns and a blood-stained robe. "Turn back!" they whispered to travelers.

Dead leaves crunched under Christian's feet. The riverbed nearby was dry. Odd echoes proliferated through the territory. Once in a while, Christian saw a shack or two, but each appeared abandoned.

* * *

One shack Christian saw was different, though. A woman and a man outside who obviously didn't want to be seen were attempting to run back into their hovel. They slammed the door behind them, then went to one of the broken windows and peered through it, like scared animals.

Christian thought that strange but continued on nevertheless. The next dwelling he came upon looked so neglected that he wondered how it would indeed be possible for anyone to live there. A frail, grizzled, ungroomed man anxiously looked out his window. He cranked it open.

"So you come without a crowd to back you up?!" the man hollered, in a sarcastic, muted voice, as if he were angry but trying to keep his volume down. "How dare you! We've all had enough already." He motioned for the boy to get out of his forest.

"Yes, I come alone, sir," Christian answered. He took off his helmet in a gesture of peace.

"Hmmm. . . on your own, eh?" the man asked again. "Because there is *always* some sort of public spectacle," he said, looking around with suspicion.

He was quick to add, "Listen, boy, I don't know what you're doing, but I know you don't belong here. Go away," he whispered harshly.

The warrior-boy raised his palms in consternation, hoping for a reason for this hostile reception.

The man stared with malignity.

"Sir, I assure you, I won't bother anyone. I was just hoping to pass through. There aren't any alternate routes. I'm sorry. . ."

Christian was still confounded, but he listened as the pathetic man went on. "Listen, nobody just passes through here, unless you're one of 'Them.' So it may appear you aren't one of 'Them.' But perhaps they are somewhere close by, waiting to sneak up on us. . ."

This talk scared Christian. He wanted to inquire about who the mysterious "Them" could be, but the man went right on talking.

"Still, no one told us you were coming. . . We always know when we're about to get a new resident, because of all the rumors."

"I'm on my way to the Celestial City. *That's* where I'm going to live," said Christian.

This last comment went right over the man's head.

"You look like nothing bad could ever happen to you. Boy oh boy, you look young, healthy, and strong. But we, we've all done, or been accused of, something awful and had to live with it, right here, for years." He revealed this with an unsettling candor, a mass of insecurity in his voice.

"I'm far from perfect," stated Christian. "Can you tell me your story?" he ventured, innocuously.

"Well, all of us here, we've been done in. Some of us deserved it; others just got put here, ostracized. Either way, things'll never go back to the way they were before. People will never look at us the same!"

"You've said you've lived here for years. Isn't that punishment enough? Who out there would still hold your past against you??"

The man looked deeply into Christian's eyes, grabbing the boy's collar through the little window. "Do you really think that anyone could ever forgive me?" he asked in anger and shame.

"Yes, of course. Jesus forgives people all the time-- of their most heinous acts, their most despicable deeds," declared Christian. "That's what I was told. Let me come in and tell you about Him and where I'm going."

The man's demeanor relaxed. He let Christian into the squalid little abode and began questioning him with ardor. "So, tell me about this Jesus of yours. You say he'll forgive me?"

"Most certainly," said Christian, confidently.

"But, but even if I am guilty of . . .?"

* * *

Suddenly, before the man could finish, the roof of the decaying hut shook violently. The man grabbed Christian's arms in fear and clung to him.

"What was that?" Christian asked.

"Hush! That's Apollyon, the ruler of this valley. He's a monster! Keep still; he's right outside!"

The evil monster the man was speaking of was an amalgamation of animal parts: dragon wings, bear feet, and a lion mouth, made even more grotesque and unreal by having a human body. It snorted the air loudly, periodically belching small gusts of heat.

"I smell the blood of a new soul," roared the monster. Neither Christian nor the man were looking out the window. They cowered in fear.

"Come out and face your fate!" roared the monster harder, fire shooting out its snout in a wicked blast of evil energy.

Christian recognized his fear, but was also aware of his new protective gear. He got up, donned his helmet again, and went to the door. He walked out in plain sight onto the forest floor.

There, Christian for the first time laid eyes on Apollyon. The baleful creature was standing there quietly now, its dark purple dragon wings enshrouding its body. Its vampiric fangs shown through its lips as it spoke. "Unlike what my dear man has just told you, we welcome you to our little den of iniquity-- wholeheartedly! You do so belong here, my dear boy! You're just the right material!"

Christian was taken aback. Immediately, he didn't like the creature's wily, sinister tone. The monster suddenly spread out its enormous wings, in a flash, to scare him. Christian jumped back a bit.

Quietly, Apollyon went on. "In fact, you're fallen, and that's our number-one requirement. God doesn't want you now. You looked with lust in your eyes at his little doll Discrecion, and you've accepted armor that doesn't belong to you. You've also been talking to one of the world's worst sinners just now-- Tch, Tch, Tch--and that's just within the last few hours." Apollyon laughed maliciously.

Christian had to agree. He felt bad that he had stirred up trouble here. In fact, he thought, maybe God had planned for him to come to this end. In addition to what the monster said, he had, after all, lost his letter and allowed it to become torn. He had wasted valuable time looking for it on the hill. He had disrespected his mother's wishes by leaving. He had stolen that toy from the department store when he was little and treated his grandfather less than respectfully more than a few times. He wasn't even sure if he hadn't been the one responsible for driving his father away.

The monster stood there, watching Christian crumble, smacking its fiery lips, ominously stroking its clawed feet on the ground. *He's mine*, thought the demon to itself.

Chp. 18: **"Beaten, Bloody, and Bruised"**
"The wages of sin is death." [Romans 6:23]

"Get on my back, and I will take you to my lair," said the monster in the sweetest tone it could muster, though still dripping with outright virulence. Every cell in its body was pounding out waves of ill will.

Christian stood still as a rock. *None of my mistakes*

has power over me anymore, he realized, remembering the Holy Ghost having taken the backpack. *Don't listen. Don't do it!* his steely resolve entreated. "Get behind me, Satan!" he screamed, with all the lung power he had. *That's what Grandpa said Jesus once said to the devil.*

It seemed to have hurt Apollyon, because the monster cupped its ears, cringing and crouching. But then it stood up quickly, an unmistakable gleam of hate in its eye, and hurled a jet of flame toward Christian. The force of it blew the boy backwards, but he was unscathed, the shield and the helmet having done their job well.

Christian then boldly ran at the monster, jumping high into the air and kicking him as hard as he could. The monster, stunned, realized this would be no easy battle. It wiped blood off its lion's mouth and lunged toward Christian, stopping just inches short of contact.

"Ssstop fighting me!" it said through sinuses full of blood. "You have no other choice than to join me now."

Give no answer, thought Christian. *Just act.* He seized the rod of Moses, transformed by Watch into a razor-sharp spear. He raised it to impale the monster through the heart, but Apollyon caught the boy's wrist in mid-air.

"I wouldn't do that if I were you," snarled the vicious monster. "I might get it, then stab you. Besides, you couldn't kill me if you tried. I don't *have* a heart!" Apollyon released his hold and laughed with reverberations, the sound of pure evil carrying on over the land.

Christian went on slashing. He ripped the spear mightily through one wing, causing a sizeable gash.

"Foolish boy!" roared Apollyon, knocking the weapon out of his hand. Christian watched in horror as it fell into a nearby well, forever out of reach. "You see!? You are too young and small to make any difference here!"

The monster grabbed the boy's arm, twisting it brutally behind him.

Pushing Christian hard against the shack, Apollyon pinned him there, no mercy. The monster intensified the awful press, and the tension on the beams rose unbearably. The shack then gave way completely, leveled like cardboard. The force had propelled Christian violently. Shoved to the ground face-first, Christian imagined the pain of the man still inside.

The monster flew over to Christian and hovered above him. It took its foot and drew its bear claw down the length of Christian's calf, to make a permanent mark of its sovereignty, to brand him as its own. Blood rose to the skin's surface in deep, crimson tracks, each one a nick in the boy's self-esteem.

Run away! was Christian's next thought, but he remembered his promise to stay brave. He rolled over and resumed fighting. He grasped his crusader's club and approached Apollyon for a devastating, heavy blow. The monster reeled backwards, its head circling and wings expanding as it tried to steady its balance. It blasted another hellish fireball from the incinerator that was its mouth, and Christian was scalded where his clothing had been torn to threads.

Much fatigued from the violence, Christian faded, and the club fell out of his hands. His strength was disappearing faster than he could strategize. A drop of liquid agony rolled out from his swollen eye, and Apollyon was right there to catch it.

"Aw, poor little Christian boy," the monster hissed, examining the tear, now crystallized in evil. "So your savior has abandoned you. Regretful, but no surprise. He never shows up when needed. . ." The creature derided Christian with raw animosity. The words infuriated the boy. Retrieving the club, he came charging and smashing, but the monster grabbed it as if it were a matchstick and threw it way off to the side.

Christian had one weapon left: the gun, a sharp shooter's rifle that had deterred a presidential assassin. He retreated some steps and took it from his belt. He aimed at the creature's brain, but it dodged to the side with inhuman speed, the bullet penetrating a nearby tree.

The monster sneered. "Target practice?" It was going to breathe fire at the gun, to melt it into a deformed, useless lump of metal.

But before that could happen, at point blank range, Christian blew a chunk out of the monster's human flesh. Blood squirted out in long arcs of red. The monster gasped in disbelief, then grasped its gouged side, assessing the massive injury. It looked at Christian as if to say "How could you?!" and stopped moving then.

Instinctively, Christian stepped forward, as if to help, transferring the gun to his other hand. But the monster recoiled and lashed out again, this time with incredible vengeance. It flew up high, high into the air and swooped down like thunder, ferociously.

Christian seized its paw quickly with his free hand, the dominant one, but a claw gored his palm, the venom released from the creature's nails stinging horrifically.

No time for pain, Christian shouted, "I call on the King!" and shot with his bloody hand rapidly, repeatedly. One bullet, precise and God-driven, hit the monster's forehead. Strangely, no blood flowed, but a rim of black powder encircled the hole. The creature's eyes crossed, and it couldn't see straight. It was grabbing futilely for the boy, who was outmaneuvering it easily.

It tried to look down again at the wound in its side, which must have caused worry, because it abruptly flew up and away, clumsily.

"Sweet victory!" shouted Christian. "Thank you, Savoir," he added, dropping to his knees, the ground saturated red through and through.

Chp. 19 **"Shadows of the Pit"**
"Rejoice not against me, O mine enemy! When I fall, I shall arise." [Micah 7:8]

Christian recalled the awful battle and hoped that it would all be behind him. *But would the monster's injuries prove to be fatal?* Though it seemed likely, Christian had no way of knowing; the dastardly creature had returned to its secret lair miles and miles away.

Then suddenly, he jumped up. *I've got to go back and rescue that man, that man inside the house,* Christian remembered. He looked at the flattened, miserable shack.

But first things first! He inspected the extent of his bodily damage. He had deep cuts in his hand, calf, and cheek, burns all over his limbs, and his muscles throbbed with excruciating pain. He rallied himself to try and tend his wounds, but he had nothing with which to soak up the thick, coagulating ooze of blood and tissue. He dragged himself to the nearby door of a different shack, but the occupant wouldn't open. In fact, the door had been barricaded, so Christian had no other choice but to go on.

He continued to force himself on his hands and knees. Since his good hand had been punctured in the attack, his weaker hand was bearing the burden of each pull. The trail had become so indistinguishable now that he had to clamber over the twisted roots of trees. The scraping to his skin wasn't allowing scabs to form. Each thrust caused more blood to spill, and a long, horrific maroon smear marked his struggle on the forest floor.

Soon, there were no more shacks. Alone and without much hope, Christian's body gave out. He lay there on his back, surveying the dark forest canopy in utter exhaustion.

I've just seen the true face of evil, he realized with a stark pang. Like the valleyfolk, he knew he would never again be the same. His childhood innocence was gone, and he had been dragged down; he was transformed—a man now—or was he a brute? He had been initiated into the ways of Satan, and it was nothing but bad news.

There was one small break in the canopy so that Christian could see by moonlight. He lifted his head slightly. A large, silvery pool of blood was collecting under his leg. Seeing that, he was morbidly astonished, and went into a state of shock. *Oh God, is this feeling my body slipping away from me? . . .*He felt badly that his mother would never be able to find his body if he were to die in a place like this.

Just then, however, a tiny ball of light with a tail of stardust dropped from the opening in the treetops. Christian was able to follow it with his eyes, with his last bit of strength. It landed on a small leaf about a foot away from Christian's outstretched, mutilated hand. The next thing he knew, Christian was holding the orb, so warm and magical, which was guiding him to a shining, green tree, apparently the one to which the leaf belonged.

The tree suddenly changed yellow-gold. *Didn't it?* Hundreds of golden leaves began falling, and Christian basked in the energy as they showered him. As the ball of light melted in his hand, the leaves excreted a heavenly balm that mended all Christian's wounds. Christian thought he could actually feel the healing process of his physical body. His head was still swirling from shock, however, his brain weaving in and out of consciousness.

"It's the Tree of Life, " said someone, who had suddenly appeared in the midst of the forest valley, the scene of so much needless destruction and fear. *Was it Evan? His grandfather?*

"And time heals all wounds," the being added, bending low to softly brush Christian's hand. *Or maybe it was nothing,* Christian thought a moment later, when the presence was no longer there.

* * *

It didn't matter that much, though, because Christian had been completely restored by the life force, concentrated in a divinely-designed warp in time. There was absolutely no trace of further blood loss, though scars remained. The confusion was also wiped away. He stood up feeling months older, and marvelous.

It was early morning, sweet springtime in the valley now, reassuring butterflies and birds in the sky. Although his clothes were thoroughly stained with blood and ripped, he still had his gun, helmet, and protective vest and was able to proceed pain-free on his mission.

Christian, the boy-turned-man warrior who had survived an encounter with the worst being of all the Underworld, Apollyon, marched through the valley for several hours, thinking: *There will be more.* The path was inclining.

The stalwart pilgrim plodded onward and eventually came to the incline's end. He marched on level ground now, ready, in the mature sense of the word, for any adventure in the name of righteousness.

* * *

It wasn't too long before he found that next adventure. It all started when he heard a bizarre, communal wail, pulsating, never subsiding. It worried him and made him feel nauseous. Christian wondered what the sickening, ongoing sound could be.

At the end of the level plane was another depression in the landscape. It was much deeper, a low chasm worse than the preceding valley. Suddenly, the moon eclipsed the sun, and Christian's world was eerily dark. All that remained was a thin, dismal halo of sunlight. He saw the mouth of a cave, with the path leading inside it at a downward angle. Christian knew right away that this must be where he would discover the source of the droning sound. Again with no knowing, he was going into the unavoidable Valley of the Shadow of Death, in which resided a whole host of monsters, including goblins, satyrs, and demons. The din and chaos as he entered were extreme.

The monsters, less lethal than Apollyon, were much smaller; nevertheless, they swarmed around Christian's head and bothered him greatly. They circled menacingly, and it was fortunate that he couldn't see them very well, inside this place of constantly shifting shadows, or he would have been much more afraid.

As he swatted at them, he realized that they were slowing his progress considerably. From time to time, they pecked at his exposed skin with their talons. They also spared none of their foul language, curses, and threats. Christian felt as though they were the most irksome creatures he had ever had to tolerate.

The dirty, rocky, lousy excuse for a trail continued on, although it was very wide and spacious. Christian could see a barbed-wire fence in the distance with a crowd of people hanging onto it inside its parameters. There seemed to be a thousand souls living there underground in loud, miserable pandemonium, all pushing against each other in an effort to get out.

Christian walked up to the fence, wanting information regarding his whereabouts.

"You're here! You're here!" scoffed one of the souls, dressed in a gray shroud, skipping around hysterically. She was smashing against the others, her voice drowning in the cacophony.

"Will you be dwelling amongst us?" shrilly shouted another, dressed in a similar burial cloth. Her shape was being distorted by shadows.

"What is this place?" screamed Christian, hoping that he were in a nightmare and not reality.

A third soul in the group pushed forward. Her face filled with a rush of pure malice. "The man you forgot about in the hut is dead!" she said with a slow, grinding tone. "You were there when he got crushed, and you didn't even care! . . He's here-- in Hell-- with us now! See him?" She was now high-pitched and petulant, pointing to a figure past some rocks, between several small, spitting fires.

Christian could see a man's shape and withdrew in dread and confusion. It was all coming back to him. He had forgotten the man in the shack!-- the man whom he had hoped would get forgiveness. He didn't really recognize this soul for sure among the flickers and shadows, but he still had a terrible feeling in his heart. *Is this true?* thought Christian. *Am I responsible?*

Chp. 20: "23"
"Pray at all times in the Spirit, with all prayer and supplication." [Ephesians 6:18]

Without any more conversation, Christian ran back to the path, trying to ignore what he had just seen. After a few minutes, he could no longer see the figure or the fence. But again, he had to stop. He felt annihilated by guilt.

He called up every muscle in his body to move forward, and he advanced a few paces. Now, the trail narrowed tremendously, without warning. He was trying to balance on a ledge no more than a foot wide. It was almost like a tight-rope.

The ledge became harder to negotiate, and the space in front of him grew pitch-black. It made him claustrophobic, maddeningly sick. Christian had to proceed slowly and with utmost caution. He put one foot in front of the other, touching the back of his heel to the tips of his sneaker toe behind. He took a few steps and almost fell off. This wasn't going to do; he would have to crawl the rest of the way. He decided to pray for help. *But what prayer to say?* Words he had heard his grandfather say hundreds of times swiftly came to mind:

The Lord is my shepherd, he thought, on his hands and knees, *I shall not want.* He remembered how before he had become a Christian he had wanted, and wanted a lot. Now, in the ultimate place of death, nothing mattered except escape. He had never wanted out of a place so badly. *Maybe speaking out loud would ward off some evil spirits and help me get out faster,* he reasoned.

So aloud, boldly, he said, "He makes me lie down in green pastures," though with a tone of denial, thinking there would be no possible way he could lie down on this stony, perilous ledge.

"He leads me beside still waters." He could smell the sulfur and hear its turbulent flow on either side of him.

"He restoreth my soul," Christian said, doubtfully.

"He leads me in the paths of righteousness, for His name's sake," he said, almost losing his footing.

"Ye, though I walk through the Valley of the Shadow of Death, I will fear no evil, for Thou art with me," Christian carried on. He heard loud, anonymous screeching, abject laughing, a hurl of insults.

"Thy rod and thy staff, they comfort me." He remembered Evan and his cane, though even that may not have helped here.

"Thou preparest a table for me in the presence of mine enemies," he said with fake force, pretending he felt reassurance from the words, but still groping wildly. He put the next knee tentatively in front of the other.

"Thou anointest my head with oil." At that moment, a winged creature swooped down, scraping his head. The blood felt oily.

"My cup overflows." Christian felt the waves of anxiety wash over him. Petrified, he vomited over the side.

"Surely goodness and mercy shall follow me all the days of my life," he went on, though it had felt that only evil had been following him as of late.

"And I shall dwell in the House of the Lord forever." With that resounding last line, bitter irony pierced his soul. The words didn't seem to be working. Christian closed his eyes in grief, wondering if he had come this far believing an empty promise.

Utterly frightened to the very core, he simply could not go on. He had reached rock bottom, paralyzed and alone in the deepest realm of evil. He even considered calling for Apollyon to rescue him; he was so far from the hill with the angels.

Suddenly, Evan's voice called out from the blackness. Evan himself was apparently on the path, several feet ahead. "Don't believe the lies of the beings down here!" he yelled. "Apollyon, not you, killed that man from the valley. And that man isn't here! He's in the Lord's House as we speak!"

There was no sound from Christian.

"OK, so you hesitated and forgot, but don't you get it?!" shouted Evan. "Remember what Gooden told you about the person who'd get rid of your sin? Remember what Interpretern told you about Passion and Patience having wanted to see the King? Well, the King, the Lord; Christ, Jesus, God; they're all one in the same! He's the ruler of the Celestial City! It's where people who believe in Him go!"

Christian was sobbing now, desperately hoping all this was true.

"You were able to speak to that man just long enough to enable him to believe, so he's there, in the City, already! And the King will bless us too one day with the undeserved destiny of eternal life in Paradise! He's vanquished sin and death, Christian. So don't worry. You will not end up here. You are on your way out. No one has any power over His will here, Christian,—or anywhere, for that matter-- not those souls, not these creatures, not even Apollyon!"

Just then, a raging demon howled and knocked Christian off balance, so that he fell over the edge. Luckily, God's presence truly *was* with Christian, and he was able to grab onto a root. Christian nervously scrambled back up over the ledge and straddled it, out of breath, just as the root pulled out.

When he got back onto his knees again, ever so carefully, he sensed, to his chagrin, that Evan had disappeared. But Evan had given Christian just enough courage to move on.

* * *

Time wore on, though he had no sense of it. His ankles were shaky, and his focus was breaking. Balancing was difficult, excruciating, while shooeing away pests in vain. A satyr shrieked. A goblin spat. Flying fiends continually buffeted his head.

Christian repeated his grandfather's psalm over and over with vehemence, for hours it seemed, galvanizing his spirit with each verse. Before long, the incline of the path was going up, and the darkness was receding. He noticed that he hadn't felt or heard a creature besiege him for some time. His limbs were now enjoying a wider berth, and he was able to stand up again. Upon leaving the cave, he was, in fact, emerging from the harrowing valley of shadows, and he knew he'd be OK now, because the sky was once more visible and the old cement walls rose up to comfort him.

Part 3: The World

Chp. 21 "Watcher"

"The dog is turned to his vomit again, and the sow that was washed to her wallowing in the mire." [2 Peter 2:22]

    Christian checked his certificate. It was safe and sound. He continued walking. Neither the sun nor moon was to be seen, so he had no idea what time of the day or early evening it was. The only atmospheric indicator was an omnipresent cloud that covered the flat, featureless land with a brooding gloom.

    Christian had the slight feeling that someone was watching him, though he saw no one. An overwhelming, unexplainable feeling of paranoia filled him as he trudged on.

    Soon, he came to an ultra-modern structure built by some commercial titan. Its sleek chrome and black reflective exterior butted up to one of the old path's walls, where the wall had been partially knocked down. Although there was no signage to the building, Christian jumped over the damage and went in, denying a little voice in his gut that said no.

    Right inside the entrance was placed an enormous plasma TV, and in its picture sat a gangly, ill-proportioned, decrepit being of some sort, covered in wrinkles. His limbs were scrawny, like sticks; his head size was astounding; his face was deformed, reptilian. He was gurgling up a putrid green foam from his mouth, and it was spilling out onto his chest. He was ogling Christian intently with protuberant eyes, leaning forward over his fat belly as far as he could.

    Christian was startled when the aberrant life form somehow pressed the screen outward, from the inside of the

TV. It stretched and swelled, extending out in three-d. *Nice trick*, thought Christian. Thankfully, there was a red velvet theater rope stretched across the picture. *It's probably supposed to be there to restrain the thing.*

There were words on a placard propped up beside the TV: "Freak Show Exhibit #1: The World's Creepiest Cannibal, Prioccupachian." A mammoth heap of bones lay nearby.

How is he able to eat people if he's not even real? wondered Christian.

"He's real, all right!" came the close-captioned script banner rolled across the bottom of the screen.

OK, maybe he's real, posed Christian in his mind, *but I bet it's just a recording.*

"This is NOT a recording," the mind-reading, scrolling banner insisted.

"How do you eat people, then?!" Christian yelled out loud. Apparently, the sickly specimen, though alive, was on mute. It continued to just sit there, watching him, watching him. Christian watched it watching him. Christian felt strange—compelled, controlled. He felt as though he were being forced closer and closer to the screen. When he was about an inch away, he resisted with all his might, and the compulsion burst like a blister.

Suddenly, the screen became like a mirror, flashing a reflection of Christian, only a hideous version. Christian's eyes were bulging and bloodshot. His teeth were black with decay. His skin was a sick bluish color, his lips an unhealthy shade of dark red. There were boils on his face.

Christian jumped backwards, appalled. He immediately checked his face with his fingers; everything felt normal enough. "Uggh"! he screamed in anger and bewilderment. "My God," cursed Christian, "is this a show for me or that *thing*?. . . "

The cannibal grinned and clapped its fat hands, like a two-year-old.

*　*　*

Some background on the cannibal: This ancient thing, having gone insane centuries before, had been in the habit of stalking travelers from his spot in a crevice in the mountainside. However, when one day a traveler came along carrying a television set, the creature became so enamored of it that he got stuck inside. (You see, TVs are ever so much more enticing than rocky crevices.)

Currently, although viewers ate up his life, so to speak, by gawking at him for cheap amusement, he always had the last laugh: he ate up the lives of the viewers, in more ways than one, exacting a fitting revenge.

You see, his glare was obtrusive, even painful, and had the power to hypnotize. Once transfixed in an immovable trance, the viewer would be drawn into the TV, like a magnet. Inside with the ogre, they would waste away. Those unlucky enough to have allowed their morbid fascination get the better of them expired after a few days. Prioccupachian would then have his meal of succulent, freshly-dead flesh, and cast the rest aside, accumulating his cache of calcium trophies.

Of course, there had been no one to explain all of this to Christian, and he had been duped once again. Yes, the age-old ogre had hypnotized him as it had so many other unsuspecting folk. But the angel on the first hill who had drawn the cross on Christian's head had put a shield of protection around him specifically for this sordid encounter. So, even though his eyes had wandered, he himself had stayed put. (He had no idea that he had so narrowly avoided this horrific fate, just like many of us don't ever know what God has kept us from, the awful things that might have been.)

*　*　*

Although that encounter should have been enough, Christian began to explore elsewhere in this fascinating mecca of cutting-edge technology. The rope from Prioccupachian's virtual exhibit trailed on, curving around a sign with an arrow on it, pointing the way to additional curiosities.

Christian looked down an endless corridor, its floor of sand, and observed an infinite number of cubicles baking under searing-hot, florescent sunlamps. Each station had a user fixated on a computer screen, drooling profusely and lasciviously at the mouth. While it appeared that millions were doing this, there were thousands in a similarly dry room just behind them who were hacking into these very same computers, spying on their neighbors' cyber activities, even writing up emails to blackmail them. Without water, the ones who had been there a while were dropping like flies.

There were other major attractions in the monstrous multi-media center. In one wing, children sat willingly strapped down to angular seats in isolation booths with huge video game consoles. The seating resembled electric chairs. Paradoxically, the more the children's bodies ached, the more they enjoyed themselves, until they could not move, think, nor speak anymore.

In another area, people in lab coats were training others how to breed computer viruses and send them like progeny out into the world. Little did they know that each night, the complex was purposely seeding the desktops' fans with spores of deadly microbes.

The part most prized by the complex's planners was its Cinema 2007. (That wasn't the year, mind you--that was the number of projection rooms it held.) Within individual theaters, films featured all kinds of living things being exploited for show, an electronic carnival of sorts gone gross and grisly. There were naked bodies engaged in unnatural acts and scenes of unholy violence. Those in the audience were laughing uproariously, pointing, making crude comments, enjoying themselves to the hilt. While they did this, there was a person there recording *them,* a voyeur secretly video taping, creating his own private peep show.

What a waste of time, Christian thought to himself, coming to his senses. He ran out of the sprawling building as fast as he could, disgusted and revolted by the entire soul-sucking production.

Chp. 22 "Friends"
"The wise shall inherit glory, said Solomon, but shame shall be the promotion of fools." [Proverbs 3:35]

Back on The Way, Christian kept running, hoping to dispel his recent memories from his mind. He had been through so much in just a few days since having read his grandfather's book. *Or was it months?* Just then, there was a break in the clouds, and Christian could see it was daytime.

He saw a figure on the path ahead of him. Christian could make it out to be a female form. He yelled for the person to stop, but she did not. Instead, she turned and shouted: "I can't stop; evil is after me!" She had long, blonde hair that swirled out into the air when she turned.

So Christian sped up, and within a few minutes, he was walking beside an old acquaintance from his hometown. Fondly, he remembered her name was Faith. But her shout had troubled him. *Did she think he was evil? Or had Apollyon returned?*

"Christian," she began, "when you ran away from Deastrukshun, your mother and brother told some people, and they started talking. It was all over town; everybody knew. I always thought about leaving; I just never did. But when you left, you got me thinking again . . so thanks, Christian. I'll get to safety now."

Christian smiled. "Well, you're welcome, friend. Did anyone else from the city come?"

"Not that I know of," Faith rejoined. "They all thought you were ill—crazy, you know. Sorry, Christian."

"Say, if you left *after* me," said Christian, "how'd you manage to get *ahead* of me? Didn't you go up those two killer hills and through those two terrible valleys?"

"Yes," answered Faith. "I went through them, since that's the only way this path goes."

The pair continued to walk on the even roadway while comparing notes about their parallel experiences. Faith hadn't fallen into the Slew, or wandered off to Reltivismville, so that had saved her precious time. Her journey had been a little bit easier because she had been a Christian for longer and was better disciplined to make good decisions.

"You've made good choices, *and* good time," Christian complimented her.

"Thanks, but it was still very difficult, as you know. It *is* very difficult, just being alive."

"Tell me about it. . ." Christian half joked. He was relieved to hear that even long-time Christians faced struggles.

The two continued walking together on the narrow roadway. They felt good in between its high cement walls. Faith felt she could trust Christian just fine.

* * *

"Christian," Faith began again, elaborating a little, "when I was in that first valley with all those hermits in the huts, I didn't meet up with Apollyon like you did, but I did have an upsetting brush with someone named Shane Shayme. He tried to humiliate me. He dug up dirt; he somehow knew about some things I had done in the past, little things."

"I had never seen them in that light, the spin he put on them. He painted such an ugly, twisted picture. The way he talked, he was trying to convince me it was real, my true identity, and that everyone knew and cared. He bullied me if I didn't turn back. He threatened me with going to get the media--he had a letter written about me full of slanderous statements--he's probably put it all over the Web by now."

Christian looked into her eyes, which were welling up with tears. "He tried to make me feel so terrible about myself—lower than low. That's why I didn't slow down when you first called me. I was hoping it wasn't him or one of his crowd catching up! I was embarrassed, Christian, and ashamed. I'm sorry."

"Oh, poor girl," said Christian, stopping to embrace her. "I wish you never had to go through that. There're lots of people out there who are filled with such hate. It doesn't surprise me what Shayme did to you. Just look at what they did to so many in the past." Faith's cross necklace gleamed in the sun.

The pair of travelers knew it was only a matter of time before their next meeting with someone on the path. Whether it would be good, bad, or indifferent, they had no idea, but they knew they would brave it together.

Chp. 23 "All Talk and No Action"
"They say and do not, but the kingdom of God is not in word, but in power." [Matthew 23:3; I Corinthians 4:20]

The clouds had lifted and it was a gorgeous day

now, the sun streaming on Christian and Faith as they ambled along in contentment. There were white and yellow flowery weeds all along the base of the roadway walls.

It wasn't long after they met up that Faith noticed a figure far off in the distance. "Hold up!" she cried.

The person waited, to their surprise. Christian and Faith galloped till they caught up with the traveler.

"Well hello!" said the man. "Such a rare treat to see someone else on this unpopular road!"

"Ah, yes," said Faith. "We two, in fact, just met up a little way back there. We had been traveling for days separately and haven't seen many others going our direction either."

The three smiled at each other, gaining strength in numbers. "Are you a Christian?" all asked simultaneously.

They laughed at the delicious synchronicity of their words and nodded their heads affirmatively. But that was the longest that their new traveling companion could evidently keep quiet. He was overflowing with excitement, and Christian and Faith found this to be a breath of fresh air.

"It's so great to find other people who believe in the King!" the man exclaimed, with the pace of a tornado. "It's really great to talk about religion, you know! I think it's just great! It always makes me so personally happy to talk about good things! Good things are what make life worth living, I think! I have always thought that it's important to have good things in your life, because, without the good things the King gives us, what else is there? Hmm? Hmm?"

But this man didn't wait for a reply; he just barreled on with his rapid-fire jabbering. "The reason why I think it is so good to discuss these things is that they make our lives so much better! The main point of religion is to enrich our lives, don't you think?"

Again, he didn't pause for any kind of reaction, or
even turn his head to look. He just went right on, faster
than an auctioneer coming in for the final bid. "Talking
about one's faith is so important! You know, it's really
important to keep talking about it, even if you're a little
down. You see, you can make things up if you need to, just
so that you can keep on talking! Don't you agree that the
sound of our voices is lovely and most pleasing to God? I
know I'm right. Right? Right?"

"Besides," the chatter-box continued, "we've got to
use our mouth. God gave it to us so that we could point out
others' faults. Yesiree! It's most important for us to show
them what they're doing wrong! They've got to be told,
you know!"

Faith had some disagreement here. She tried to get
a word in edgewise, but it was too hard, because the man's
talk went right over hers like a tsunami. All that she had
managed were a few clipped grunts. She noticed that their
walking pace had increased unreasonably too.

"Yes, our best weapon is our mouth, I'd have to
say! The smartest people don't sit back, I tell you; they
express their opinions up front! I was the captain of my
debate team in high school, and it's really paid off, as you
can see! Nobody can tell me anything I don't want to hear
now! The secret is in just going on, just letting the words
flow out, just—"

But Christian was by now getting irritated, enough
to want to clobber the man. He physically stopped him in
mid-stride, grabbing him by the arm so as he'd have to
listen. "Hey, man, do you ever slow down? I mean, my
friend Faith here just tried to say something, and you
plowed right over her!" he declared in Faith's defense.

"Oh, sorry," the man said, "What was it that you
wanted to say?" He stood still for half a second.

Faith reasserted herself. "What I was trying to say
is that I'd have to disagree with a couple things you said."

"Oh ya? Like what?" the man said quickly. He had to be the fastest talker either Christian or Faith had ever heard. Christian cupped his hand over the man's mouth and held it there tightly.

"Well, for instance," said Faith, meekly, "I agree that spreading the Gospel is very important, but I think that just talking about the King isn't enough. I think that if we are filled with His spirit, we'll naturally want to do good, and those deeds we do will be the mark of our beliefs, a sign for others. You know, like the saying, it's easy to talk the talk, but to walk the walk is another story."

Their new acquaintance was having major difficulty restraining himself. He winced and wrinkled his eyebrows to express disapproval, mumbling something or other under Christian's hand. When Christian released it because of the slimy spit, the speaker took his tirade back up as if he hadn't even heard what Faith had said.

"And talking about the King and our beliefs is the best way to have a great day! So many people need to hear it!" The man began to skip along. "You know, they say that you will get in a better mood, even if you're in a bad mood to begin with, if you'll just start talking yourself into a better place—" prattled on the man repetitively. But he was forced to stop yacking momentarily in order to gasp for some air.

Christian took advantage of the man's need to breathe and added, "I think that's true—"

The man began to spew, but Faith this time clapped *her* hand over his great, jawing maw.

"-- and great advice," continued Christian, "but the part you said about the purpose of religion—just being there so we could have a better day—that's not all there is to it. It's there to lead people into relationship with God."

"My grandfather said that religion is not so important as spirituality," Christian went on, enjoying the space of silence Faith provided. "I think he meant that what you feel in your heart is more important than all the empty things people can say out loud."

Faith let go. The man, regaining the floor, so to speak, rattled off a series of additional, unrelated observations, most of which he appeared to be thinking up right then and there.

"Pardon me," interjected Faith, "But you asked what else is there besides good things." The traveler continued on, rudely, so she had to yell over him. "Well, for one, even if we don't always have good things happening to us, we have the *promise* of the King. We can't control what the world dishes out."

"That, my dear, is gobbledygook, poppycock, malarkey! You're thinking too much!" babbled the talk-driven traveler. "What we say that comes out of our mouths first and naturally is truth! Just let it flow out, like a bubbling brook! You can't be wrong if you do it that way. Speak now, think later! Now, those are some words to live by! Words to live by, I say!" He was rambling, ranting, raving.

Christian and Faith--they were correcting him, but oh, it was so difficult!

As the man bantered back and forth with Faith and Christian, what had started out as a pleasant conversation soon erupted into a shouting match.

The man began to tune his traveling partners out then completely, singing a crazy little melody made of nonsense words. It was at this point that Christian and Faith recognized the fact that they weren't dealing with someone who had all his "marbles." They looked at each other and shook their heads.

The man was clearly in his own little world now, talking to himself just as rapidly as he had begun. "My gosh, he talks a lot!" remarked Faith.

"Yeah, he won't shut up!" agreed Christian.

"But don't worry about him," Christian remarked, with further explanation. "I actually know him from before. He used to live in our city, before you came. His name is Gabby. He's always been very, very talkative. He was sort of the village clown, always on his soap box about something or other. I guess one day he got religion."

"It's a pity he can't listen to anyone else's perspective," said Faith. "Most of what I've learned I've learned from sitting back and listening to others. I guess he thinks he's got it all figured out."

"Nobody's got it all figured out," said Christian, sagely, "expect for God."

It was then that this character, twirling in desultory circles, and singing wildly to himself, departed from the pair, off the path and into the weeds. He was spinning around faster and faster, drunkenly, making no forward progress at all.

"I feel bad for him," noted Faith. "He loves to hear himself talk, but he's a man of little action. I wonder how long it will take him to catch up with us, if he ever does!"

"He may not," said Christian, with pathos.

Faith and Christian felt as if they had been through the spin cycle of the washing machine, their heads dizzy from the man's lightning speech. Some of it had made sense, some of it was hard to follow, and some of it was just plain wrong. . . .

"Come, now, my friend," said Faith, "I've heard that somewhere along this road is a mall, a beautiful place where we'll be able to rest and maybe even do a little window-shopping. I am sure we'll be able to find lots of people there, people we could talk with rationally, people who understand that a conversation is a two-way street."

* * *

It wasn't long after that that the road turned into a

highway, and the pilgrims started to see flags attached to light posts along The Way. These special, colorful banners floated in the warm, spring breeze, high up in the sky, dancing. "'Have it all!' at Vanity Faire" they boasted. Looking down the highway, Christian and Faith made note that it all was so pretty, so lively. Motorists in stylish cars were coming along, all going the same place. There was excitement in the air.

"We're going to have a wonderful time here today, Christian!" said Faith ardently.

"Maybe so!" said Christian. They thought nothing of the man some miles back, sputtering foolish gibberish, utterly lost.

Chp. 24 " 'Have It All !' "

"Yea, because he was such a person of honour, Beelzebub had him from street to street and showed him all the kingdoms of the world in a little time that he might, if possible, allure that Blessed One to cheapen and buy some of his vanities." [Matthew 4:8-9; Luke 4:5-7]

Christian and Faith approached the mall, Vanity Faire, supposedly the largest of its kind in the world. The regal colonnade at the main entrance made it the pinnacle of Western architecture, exuding a presence of profit, power, and prestige. It was not one shopping mall, but in fact several linked together by terraces, elevators, and trams. It looked as if it went on forever. Thousands of shops and stores with all the most modern glitz and glam beguiled guests. With merchandise and services for everything from taxes to tuxedoes, there was nothing this super world-inside-a-world did not offer. The enormous commercial district was said to employ over a million workers, each hand-picked for their steadfast belief in the corporate system.

It was spacious and clean and filled with the energy of eager, pumped-up people. They bustled while searching for treasure, weaving in and out of each other, most with a quick, determined stride.

What a flow of humanity! What a mass of desire! It represented those from all walks of life. Some people were leaving at the same time others were coming, and Christian could see that although the incoming looked happily expectant, those who were leaving all had huge packs to carry, most of which seemed to weigh them down a great deal.

Christian and Faith sauntered through the wide, wide halls. Piped-in background music with a quick, happy beat set the mood for a productive day of acquiring. The luxurious granite floors were a welcome change from the uneven, rocky path they had once been on.

"Do you think we are still on The Way?" asked Christian to Faith.

"There were no other roads that I could see. Maybe the King wants us to go through this for some reason," Faith postulated.

"Have it all! Have it all!" sang out one of the mall greeters. Faith was enjoying herself so far, taking in all the sights of the marketplace and its people, although she had come with no cash, and knew she'd not be able to make any purchases.

Christian pointed out a place with mannequins in the front that looked just like Worldly Wiseman. He looked wistfully at the models' sharp clothes, especially since he knew his ruined clothes and strange military gear were making people stare.

Faith noticed a nail salon. Girls and women were crowding each other to get into the place. There were hundreds of appealing colors of nail polish along the interior.

Next along the concourse was an eatery with floor-to-ceiling windows. Christian and Faith were quite hungry. Customers were lying down to eat, and conveyor belts carrying food aplenty rolled around them. It was a smorgasbord of all-you-can consume delicacies. Christian and Faith looked at the diners in envy.

A casino was the next establishment along the route. People were pulling levers and throwing dice. Christian and Faith could see people thrusting their arms up in frustration, and others leaping into the air in glee.

Gold coins spit out and covered one player. A giant gold dollar sign on ropes came down from the ceiling, and a loud buzzer went off. Balloons and confetti spilled from the air, and a chorus of girls came over chanting "Winner! Winner!" The man was swooping up the coins into his arms, enthralled in rapture, kissing the money like a fool.

Children around him were attempting to steal whatever their little hands could hold, while just five feet away, almost invisible, another man was reaching for a razor blade. . . He had lost his life savings, or so it had said on a huge, electronic sign revealing it to the world. His grief was overpowering.

Just then, one of the winner's stray coins rolled out the door and came to rest near Christian's foot. He picked it up and inspected it, a look of doubt spreading over his face. "Twenty years ago," said Christian to Faith, "my grandfather said, money used to say 'In God We Trust.' Now it's just got a picture of the Faire; no words, just numbers. I guess times have changed." He put the coin back onto the ground, slowly. A child ran to it and greedily pecked it up.

"Let's move on," said Faith, with rue.

"Have it all! Have it all!" a chorus of clerks chirped

in the front entrance of a nearby infants' clothing store.
Mothers were inside, busily dressing up their tiny babes in
all sorts of outlandish outfits, flashing them in front of
mirrors, as if the babies could appreciate the coming
expenditures. One mother fiercely grabbed the last outfit
of its kind right out from another.

Christian and Faith then came by a window through
which they could see workers in white coats milling about.
The sign above their establishment read "Plastic Surgery
While You Wait." Faith, touching her shallow cheekbones,
considered the plainness of her looks. She approached the
counter and asked what services were available. "Here's
one of our brochures," said the receptionist.

"Thank you," answered Faith.

"Have it all! Have it all!" the receptionist added in
automatic response.

Christian and Faith sat on a bench near a beautiful,
bubbling fountain, and Faith examined the literature, while
Christian watched the clerks count wads of cash. Faith
read. "Nose jobs, lip and calf enhancements, lipos, you
name it."

The two looked up from their seat to see a woman
strutting out with bandages all over her head. On her chest,
she proudly wore a complimentary sign from the spa that
read, "Jane Doe Today; Your Date Tomorrow." Another
person came out, this time a man. He looked exactly like
the leading actor on Christian's favorite TV show. Then
another man came out just a minute later, looking identical
to the first. "Faith," said Christian, "please promise me
you'll always look like yourself. The King made you
perfect as you are."

"I was just about to say that to you, Christian," she
answered, depositing the pamphlet in the trash.

The pair walked on. The crowds of people were
getting thicker, jostling Christian and Faith around from
time to time uncomfortably. A little boy behind them with

his mother was whining about getting a video game, and a teenager was protesting into her phone about having to go home for dinner.

A man on a platform was calling out. "White picket fences for sale, white picket fences! All your neighbors have got'em! Stay up with your neighbors! Have it all!" Christian noticed that the man's lapel had a name tag that read "Mr. Jones" on it.

For quite a few hours, Christian and Faith explored Vanity Faire, bombarded with all its novelties and attractions. In addition to the big department stores, there were innumerable panderers of all kinds stationed in the corridors, hawking their wares like the man on the platform. Some sellers were quite aggressive, even pushy. Several times as the teens were walking by booths, the seller would yell something to Faith or Christian, tempting them with products supposedly to make them more desirable, happier, healthier, more 'complete.' But each time they were approached in this way, Christian and Faith politely said 'no.'

"Have it all! Have it all!" bellowed a man with a security guard's suit on as he walked parallel to the two. He lowered his voice for a minute and peered directly at Christian and Faith. "Well, folks, seems as though we haven't found what we're looking for," he said, the slightest tinge of disgust in his tone.

"We're just browsing, thanks," said Faith.

"Well, I'm sure you'll come across it soon. Everyone does!" He began to walk the other way, not without stealing a backwards glance at the couple.

"That was weird. . .," said Christian.

* * *

After a while, they came upon a place that looked busier than even any of the restaurants, located on the perimeter of the complex. It had drive-in bays, like in an automotive garage. But it wasn't just cars that were coming in, or fast food that was going out. It was a body business. A sign overhead said, "Cremation while you wait. $10 per body." Near it, another sign read, "Trash disposal provided, no extra charge." People were coming up to the counter, paying the fee, and leaving within minutes, rubbing their hands together in expeditious finality. It didn't settle well with Christian and Faith, but everybody else acted as if it were normal.

The two went on. They saw fluffy wigs, bejeweled gowns, speed boats, robotic irons, iron-clad security systems, and such. After hours of marveling at all the new high-tech inventions and gadgets, as well as the latest must-have improved products, Faith and Christian had the melancholy feeling that they themselves were lacking.

"I love these pretty lip glosses," said Faith, picking up a small cosmetic. "I used to wear lip gloss on Sunday to church."

"I wish I had some money to buy you something," said Christian to Faith, but when I heard that my city was going to burn, I left with nothing, as fast as I could get going. Do you have any? Money, I mean?"

"No, my friend, I can't say as I do," she said, dejected, replacing the lipstick in its stand.

By now, it was more than just the security guard who had noticed them. They had also drawn the attention of a crowd. They could hear people whispering about them. "Look at that man, Mama!" hissed one child, easily overheard.

"They don't have any packages!" said another, outraged.

"They don't look normal!" said an older lady to her friend, speaking on the other side of the hand raised to her mouth.

Christian and Faith felt uneasy. They were being roughed up by the crowd, who had now taken on the essence of an angry beast, pointing fingers, invading their space.

Chp. 25 "But. . . ! "
"A good man shall lay up gold as dust." [Job 22:24]

As one can imagine, Faith and Christian were not getting along so well now at Vanity Faire. In fact, it wasn't long after the mob began encircling them and shoving that the security guard returned with reinforcements.

"Get back! Get back!" he boomed to the throng, pushing his way toward Faith and Christian. He grabbed and cuffed them, yanking them out of the middle. "Follow me!" he ordered.

"What's going on?" shouted Christian. "Where are you taking us?"

"You're disturbing the peace," answered the guard, brusquely.

"But we didn't do anything wrong!" yelled the pair, in unison.

"We'll just let the judge see about that!" another guard answered.

The two were led to another shop, the sign overhead reading, "Just Justice." Below the establishment's name, it read in smaller print: "Case Closed in Fifteen Minutes or It's Free!"

Christian and Faithful were mortified and frightened, but they did not lash out. "Tell us what we did wrong. Please!" Christian begged.

Inside, there was a long line of people in orange jumpsuits and handcuffs, escorted by police officers. A judge behind a walk-up counter was sentencing people every ten to twelve minutes.

When Christian and Faith reached the counter, one of the guards handed the judge a ticket. "Oh," said the judge, "Disturbing the peace, I see!"

"That's ridiculous!" said Christian, curbing his anger as much as possible. "We didn't do anything! We're innocent. The King knows we're innocent!"

"Well," laughed the judge, heartily. "The King's not here, so he appointed me! *I'm* the King here, and it's *my* court. What I say goes."

"But—" Christian insisted.

"Say one more word, and I'll hold you in contempt of court!" said the judge. He was irate now, a big purple vein pulsating in his forehead as he leaned up over the counter and banged his gavel.

A ready-made jury sitting to the side cackled back, booing the young people's plea. They looked like a pack of villains. Some were spitting at Christian and Faith, while some were throwing their pencils, sharpened to fine points. A few of the make-shift projectiles hit the defendants' skin. The jurors were also throwing vile execrations, malicious missiles of provocation. Christian and Faith felt abased, like the despised playthings of hyped-up spectators at a Roman coliseum.

Faith whispered to Christian in all the mayhem. "Don't worry, sweet Christian," she said, tearfully, "God sees all, and he *knows* we are not guilty."

". . .And that's not all, Judge," said one of the guards loudly. "This witness here," he said, pointing to a child he had dragged along with him, "says he saw the woman put a lipstick in her pocket."

Chp. 26 " ' Justice' "

"To get widows' houses were their intent, and greater damnation was from God their judgment." [Luke 20: 46, 47]

Inside this travesty of a courtroom in Vanity Faire, Faith checked her pockets, wondering if she could have inadvertently taken the lip gloss. But nothing, of course, was there. "It's a lie!" she screamed, "a lie!"

But the severe tyrant presiding, Judge Haytewell, didn't care. He looked at his watch and at the power-hungry jury seething with rage.

"Considering the additional charge of theft, the court hereby orders you to pay a penalty of six hundred, sixty *plus six* dollars," the judge declared, opening the cash register with a ca-ching.

"What?! That's a rip off! -- What my grandfather used to call 'highway robbery'!" Christian exclaimed. "We don't have that kind of money!"

"Pay up or shut up!" yelled a guard, pulling Christian's frayed collar, ripping it along the neckline.

There was a break in the sentencing then. Christian lowered his head and moved it side to side, indicating again to the judge that he had no mode of compensation.

"Then you'll have to be retained in our detention center until someone can come bail you out."

"But we're alone, Judge! We don't have anyone who could!" said Christian, trying to restrain his indignation.

"Get them out of here!" belted out the judge, disinterested. The pair were pushed backwards, making room for the next unfortunate party.

* * *

"What a great justice system we have!" said another guard, smiling. "Works like a charm, every time."

"Works like a ch-charm?!" Christian stammered. "We didn't disturb your peace! And we didn't shoplift! I demand you let us go!"

"Ya, ya, I've heard it all before," said the burly guard. "Now, you heard the man: shut up!"

"What did we do to be considered 'disturbing the peace'!" Christian asked, ignoring the command.

"Well, you tell me!" retorted the guard.

"Nothing. . . we were just minding our own business," answered Faith, her wrists being rubbed raw by the cuffs. She and Christian were being nudged along down another hall.

"Humph!" snorted the big guard. "Seems as though your 'nothing' was quite something, something we've never seen around *here* before! You've been in here for a long time, and you don't have a single thing bought! What's wrong with you people? You're scaring our customers! You're making them think!"

"Nothing is wrong with us, sir," explained Faith. We just don't value money or possessions that much. Our main goal is to get where we're going. . . to the Celestial City."

"I knew it!" the other guard exclaimed. "Bible-Beaters! Do you know how bad for business you are? Troublemakers of the very worst kind! Get in there!" He pushed them into a dark, cold holding cell.

* * *

Hours passed. No food or drink was allowed, no succor for the weary explorers. Christian and Faith were each chained to rusty rings on opposite sides of the large, concrete cell.

A guard came in and slammed Christian on the top of the head with a book. "Here, Bible-Beater, take that!"

he scoffed, hitting him again with the heavy object. Although Faith was facing the other direction, she realized what was going on and let out an impassioned cry. Then the officer proceeded to abuse Faith the same way. Her head smashed against the wall. Her lip bled.

Over the course of a sleepless night, the pair was severely mistreated, almost tortured, you could say. They were at a loss to sufficiently explain why they had been impounded here, but they prayed together often to try and make it through.

They could hear the judge and some others talking. Intermittent phrases were wafting down through a heating vent in the ceiling.

"They're strange. . ." was perceptible.

"They're dangerous," Christian could make out.

"And they've got no money to give us. That makes them harmful *and* worthless," Faith heard. More bits and pieces of sentences came along. They recognized the words "image" and "price." Lastly, they heard this: ". . .needs to be made an example of." Both Faith and Christian got very nervous. They tried to assure each other from their helpless positions on either side of the cell.

But Christian couldn't help Faith when they came in and took her, grabbing her by the roots of her beautiful, long hair. He couldn't help her at all.

Chp. 27 "Forgive Us Our Trespasses, As We Forgive Those Who Trespass Against Us"

"Above all take the shield of faith, wherewith ye shall be able to quench all the fiery darts of the wicked."
[Ephesians 6:16]

It was the worst sound Christian had ever heard in his life, that iron door closing. Faith was gone. That night, all Christian could do was strain to listen through the air vent, hoping he could latch on to any more fragments of information about the girl.

Not long after Faith had been removed, Christian was able to hear a loud uproar coming from outside the mall. There was chanting like from a great mass of people hellbent on something. They wanted something done, and their verbal insistence was relentless.

Outside, unbeknownst to Christian, his friend's life was ending—murderously. The guards had lashed Faith to a conveyor belt usually used to take incoming shipments into the main distribution center of the mall. People surrounded the length of the belt, brandishing fiery clubs. As Faith's body proceeded from one end to the other, the blood-thirsty (self-righteous consumers, managers, store owners, and mall officials) took pleasure in maiming her sadistically. The thrill was utterly satisfying. Their death-lust and ecstasy ran high. Faith was beaten with closet rods, stabbed with fireplace pokers, stoned with paperweights, doused with accelerant, and, at the end of it all, torched to death in the drive-up mortuary's incinerator. Some sparks spewed from the exhaust pipe, flying away in the bitter, turbulent wind.

In all, she withstood it as quietly and calmly as history's humblest martyrs had, placing her faith always in something greater. But the King didn't let it pass that easily.

* * *

Christian heard the commotion eventually fade. By then, he knew something was terribly, terribly wrong. He was calling out to the name of his king. "My God, please don't let them have taken my Faith!"

It was almost dawn. Christian could hear muted laughing coming through the air duct now. "Serves her right!" someone said. It was at that moment that Christian's heart exploded into a million little pieces.

He fell unconscious, his body dangling, his wrists being held up only by the chain mounted high on the wall.

When he woke up, the thought of the probable killing hit him like a train colliding with a car stalled on tracks.

He saw a meager tray of food inside the iron door. It was a mean trick, though, because it was far out of reach. He stood up, noticing that there was no feeling in his right hand. He began to massage it as best he could.

A guard came in presently and unlocked the cuffs to allow him to eat his breakfast. Christian devoured it in thick, rapid clumps like an animal.

"They've made their decision," said the guard. "They're going to have you work off your debt."

"Never mind that! What happened to my friend?"

"Oh, she's been taken care of. . . .Did you want her ashes in an urn or scattered? I think there's a special going on right now: nine bucks for a plastic urn, or free if you turn it over for recycled packaging material."

"God! God! She's dead? Please tell me she's not dead!" screamed Christian.

"Oh, she's dead all right. She almost destroyed our whole way of life! Nothing can justify that. But everything's back in order now. There's a smooth flow of commerce. It's all good," explained the guard.

The confirmation of the death engulfed Christian.

But she'd want me to go on. . . thought Christian, stiffly, after a few moments.

"What do you mean—work off my debt?" he ventured.

"Oh, you'll see," the guard said. "Our highest company executive heard your case last night."

*   *   *

All kinds of gruesome possibilities swirled through Christian's mind—slavery in sweatshops, designed to keep Monster Materialism stoked and alive somewhere, seemed the most likely outcome.

I won't serve that master! came Christian's thought. So, with a tremendous rush of energy, he broke away from the guard and bolted down the passage.

The guard was yelling into his walkee-talkee. But Christian was way ahead, opening a heavy metal door. As the guard caught up with him, he used it to smash the guard in the face. The guard lay out cold.

Christian ran down another hall, gray, with no sign of life. There were several doors, each marked with different department names. Guards would be on his tail within seconds.

*   *   *

Arbitrarily, Christian chose the door that said "Shipping." Inside was nothing but a huge warehouse, full of boxes, no people in sight. Christian searched frenetically for an exit sign, but there was none. Exhausted and bereft over Faith's death, he fell to the floor, sure he was trapped.

He sat there on the warehouse floor not knowing what to feel. He thought of the many so eager to hate him, though none of them even knowing him. He was too full of hate to pray. *It wouldn't work anyway* came the empty thought. His faith was totally gone.

"To hell with it!" he screamed, jumping to his feet, smashing boxes, his aggression splitting at the seams. Thousands of dollars of merchandise were spilling to the floor, breaking.

When everything in his immediate range had been broken, he paused for a minute to look for his next target. He started to shake.

After one more furious, intense episode, he stopped and held his head down low in his hands. He sank down to his knees. *Nothing, nothing. . .nothing can replace her.*

* * *

Christian suddenly saw a pair of women's sandals on the floor, with soft, linen straps ending in loose bows around delicate ankles. He looked up. A teenage girl had appeared out of nowhere. She had short, dark hair and shiny, blue eyes, shiny because each held one tear that could never quite drop.

Immediately, his horrible mood began to crack.

"Take it easy; they'll hear you!" she said softly, tentatively sitting on a box.

"I heard about what happened to your friend," she said with genuine kindness. "Be strong," she urged, "because I think you will see her again someday-- that is, if you're on your way to the Celestial City. I'm Hopeful."

"Oh, you are!?" cried Christian, as sarcastically as he could. "How *can* you be?" He tensed his body.

"Shh!" she admonished him. "Because that's what my parents named me, silly."

"Oh, sorry, I see," said Christian through a shallow breath. "Your actual name is Hopeful?"

"Yes, but just call me 'Hope' for short, OK?" Even her eyes were smiling, attempting to nurse his soul.

"Now, I know that you are in a really bad place, mentally and physically, Christian. But we've got to get you out of here—and quick! That monster, Apollyon, has put a spell on this place, a kind of insurance policy in case you try and escape. He knows he killed your Faith, and without it, you are virtually helpless. But he never counted on the fact that the King would send *me*."

"The King sent you? Just for me?" asked Christian unbelieving. A small stream of blood trickled down his temple, a casualty of his rampage with the boxes.

"Uh-huh! He told me when I was praying."

Christian looked at her with mixed emotions.

"Please get up, Christian, please!" Hope whispered in urgency.

Christian looked on the scene of destruction in front of him and was embarrassed at his conduct. "I do want to go to the Celestial City still. . . I just don't know if I can."

"I'm with you now, so don't feel so bad, OK?" pled Hope, stroking his cheek. "You have me. I am your Hope." Her eyes were still glistening with tears that would not fall.

Christian extended his hand, weakly.

* * *

Just then, Apollyon's spell seemed to burst, because three Exit signs shone brightly, in places where Christian had already checked. Hope took Christian's hand, gathered all her strength, and supported him out the door, into the open air, where a fresh breeze blew into his lungs.

It was just then that a number of security guards rushed into the storage room, mad and breathless.

Chp. 28 "Identities"
"It is said of the men of Sodom that they were sinners exceedingly." [Genesis 13:13]

Out in a rear lot of Vanity Faire, Christian and Hope fled as fast as humanly possible. They pushed their legs harder and farther than at any time in their lives. They never looked back, but they heard the mall guards shouting after them, and they knew that the city authorities wouldn't be far behind.

The absconders ran to the nearest road, clearly not the walled road they'd been on, and lifted their thumbs in uncertainty, hoping to get a ride from someone. They knew hitchhiking was dangerous, but they had no choice.

Soon a van came along, painted white and black, one color each side, most curiously. It was windowless, except for the darkly tinted panes of the front.

The driver slowed down, rolled down a window, and looked at them pleasantly, motioning for them to get in. He had a plaid flannel shirt, a grisly beard, and two chipped teeth. Despite his dishevelled appearance, in the mere seconds Christian and Hope had to think, the man seemed wholesome enough; the clean, crisp morning air presented all in its best light.

Christian and Hope glanced at each other, knowing they didn't have much time. They jumped aboard through the white sliding door.

"Hey, Mister, thanks a lot," said Hope.

They made it no secret that they were in trouble. "We just came from the mall," explained Christian, "and we've got a problem."

"My friend here," Hope continued, "was arrested because he was with a friend who got framed. We've got to help him get away!"

The driver listened and sized up the situation slowly.

"Please hurry! Hurry and drive us away!" she yelled.

"Hold on, lady," said the driver, lackadaisically. "I'll go as fast as I kin, but I sure hope you ain't a-lyin'." He looked into the rear-view mirror with reservation.

Then, finding truth in their expressions, he pulled away from the curb. "Understood, folks. No worries. . ."

The driver stepped on the gas. "So, where yas two off to?" he asked.

"Anywhere, Mister," answered Christian.
"Anywhere this truck can take us, we'd appreciate, sir. I
was on my way to the Celestial City, but I know we're off
that road now. My friend—my other friend, I mean-- was
with me too, but she ended up getting k--. . ." He couldn't
bring himself to say it.

Hope comforted him, rubbing his back. "It's OK,
it's OK," she said softly.

The man looked in his rear-view mirror again,
swerving a bit. "I'm sorry, son," he offered.

"Oh, don't be sorry," Christian said with a stiff
upper lip. "If I can, I'm going to do something to make
things right," he stated, vindictive hatred in his voice, Mr.
Gooden's good will being so far removed.

"Shh!" said Hope again. "Remember what we
said."

There was a brief lull in the conversation, as the
man searched for an appropriate exit off the road. "Listen,
folks, I'm gonna try an' get yas back to that-there road to
the Slesstal City. Not sure where it is, but we'lls find it."

Hope felt good about the driver's kind words.
"Yes, let God be our driver," she said.

The three made some small talk as the van traveled
on quickly. Soon, the metropolitan feel of the area was
lessening, and it was clear that they were entering a quieter,
residential district.

"So tell me, folks, what's yer names?" the driver
asked.

"I'm Hope, and this is my friend Christian," she
answered.

"Good! I'm Byends Fairweather, but friends call
me 'By,'" said the man. He went rounding a curve at a
more leisurely speed now. "Think we'se almost there."

This doesn't look like The Way I was taking,
Christian thought with a pang. The van took several more
twists and turns.

"Uh, probly not," replied By. "I thought I could 'member where that street was, but guess I was thinkin' of some other place. Anyway, just you's jist stop at my place for a while. Nobody'll 'spect you there. You kin relax, get back on yer feet. And I kin check a map fer that road yas want. Sound good?"

Christian and Hope weren't sure, but they didn't have much to lose. They accepted the invitation readily.

The van turned a corner and pulled into the driveway of a typical looking, older house.

* * *

Inside, Byends introduced the two travelers to his roommates. "This here, these is my buds: Smoothman, Fasinbothways, Whateva, and Two-Tongues." He pointed to each one as he spoke their name.

Then he *explained* all their names. "Smoothman— we call him that 'cause a his greasy hair that keeps a-fallin' down the sides a' his head if he don't fancy-dancy mousse it." He went over and tossled the hair playfully. The others chuckled. "Fasinbothways—he got that-there name 'cause he's always poppin' this way an' that, lookin' out fer them 'po-lice,' ha ha!" Byends mimicked the ridiculous, paranoid turning motion, followed again by a snicker from the others. "Now Whateva, he got that name from his *girlfriend.*" By jutted his head side to side on his neck three times as he spoke the name's syllables with attitude. His buddies doubled over in laughter. "And Two-Tongues, well. . . jist show these-here folks yer new tongue!" The guy stuck out his tongue, wiggling it obscenely, showing that, in fact, it was surgically split.

Hope thought it was creepy; she reached for Christian's arm.

Even Christian now had qualms. *What have I gotten myself into now?* he thought as he wondered what would happen next.

After a few brotherly slaps, the gang plopped down on their couches and opened beers. Byends did the same, relaxing. He motioned for the newcomers to join them. "Take a load off," he said.

Christian and Hope sat, politely refusing any alcohol. Byends lit up, and smoke filled the room.

"These-here folks is gonna camp here awhile with us."

"Cool," said Smoothman.

"Whateva," said Whateva.

"Either way, makes no diff'rence to me," said Fasinbothways.

The men sat there, drinking and puffing. Just then, the phone rang, and the caller ID on the television read "666-6666: A." Two-Tongues went quickly out of the room to answer it.

"Hey, uh, tell 'em 'bout what happened to yas,' suggested Byends, giving Christian a cigarette.

"Uh, no thanks," said Christian, putting the cigarette down. "And if you don't mind, I'd rather not go through it again."

"He's a little shaken up," said Hope, rapidly covering for her friend.

"Sure, sure," By returned.

Christian's eyes wandered around the room. It was like a run-down funeral parlor. He was drawn to an obscure picture on the wall, of what appeared to be a Satanic symbol. . .but perhaps not; the curtains were heavy, black, and drawn, making it hard to see.

Smoothman was inhaling food, making grunting noises like a pig. In an effort to be likeable, he spit out "Mi casa es su casa" between chews. "Whatever you need, just ask Fasinbothways. He'll get it for ya."

Fasinbothways, half chuckling, half irritated, muttered, "Ya, ya," as he opened another beer and flipped the bottle cap into the air.

After a few minutes, Two-Tongues came back in the room. He clapped his hands together as if to stir up some energy. "Say, where yas off ta next-- after here, I mean?"

"They said they's goin' to the Sslestal City, is what they said," Byends answered for his guests. "We'se jist gonna git a map 'an some grub, thin head out. Yas comin' too?"

"Oh yeah," said the others.

Byends went into the kitchen to find a map. Two-Tongues followed him. When they re-emerged, Christian asked them if they had located the route.

"Ya," said Byends. "Two, he shown me jist now."

Fasinbothways stole a glimpse of Christian, darting his eyes back to the television, not wanting to be seen.

* * *

Later, the entire group boarded the van, from the black side this time. The van retraced the same side streets. The men conversed, bringing up the weather, this and that. But somehow, Christian didn't feel wholly comfortable. There was something not quite right.

The van began heading right toward the mall again.

"What are you doing?" yelled Christian. "You know that's where we were escaping from! They'll see us! Turn around!"

Byends swiveled his upper half around with an unexpected, ominous scowl. "Uh, this-here *is* the right way. That-there 'while back was Mister Apollyon himself on the phone, 'case yas didn't figure. Filled us in on who yas is."

Christian's face went white. Byends' associates stared at him, their small, colorless eyes throwing darts of hate.

Suddenly, Smoothman broke the tension. He slapped his knee and laughed, elbowing a crony. "They thought we was good guys! 'Magine that, Two-Tongues!"

Two-Tongues swore in arrogant agreement at what he found to be a hilarious arrangement of events. One of the other abductors passed gas rudely. "Ya pig!" joked another.

"So what are you going to do with us?" Hope ventured asking.

"Well, my little lady, you two is goin' right back to the big VF," said Two-Tongues. "Judge--he'll take care a yas the *proper* way this time, like yer other friend there, whatever her name was, right Whateva? . . . We's gonna have us some tasty barbeque tonight, yes sirree!"

Whateva was grabbing his sides, almost choking in vile laughter. Christian and Hope were speechless.

"Uh," went on Two-Tongues in explanation, "Mr. Ap told me 'bout your first little friend sneakin' through the Valley without meeting him. He didn't take kindly ta that, no, not 'tal. He wanted ya to know that he takes *special care* with all his guests. That's why he had 'er roasted!"

Again, a cackle of ugly laughter arose from their malicious mouths.

A debilitating sense of dread filled Christian. He felt responsible for having led Hope into this terrible quandary; he felt like the most prodigious fool in history. *I should have seen this coming. . . Whatever made me think I was good enough to enter the King's city anyway?*

* * *

Hope, after simply taking a minute to gather her thoughts, addressed the evil group. She began speaking of knowing about their great disconnect with the King, but how He still loved them so.

Their initial response was to tell her to shut up, of course. But she went right on, secure in the truth of her message. There were moments that she lost some wind beneath her sails, because of their stiff hostility, but she never let go of the rope. Her speech was impassioned.

Byends slowed the van down. Something was getting under his skin. Something Hope was saying was penetrating that thick skull of his. And all of the riff-raff were listening too.

"God didn't make you this way," she stated, rousing their emotions. "You had tough starts. Nobody's blaming you for the road you took. Your Father in Heaven doesn't care-- He just wants you back! Period!"

The henchmen's eyebrows lowered, and they soaked up her words with intensity.

"Fasinbothways," she went on, "The Devil calls you 'friend' now, but your name was Frank when you were little, wasn't it? And Whateva, your name was Winston, right?"

The two men, awestruck at this young woman's special abilities, shook their heads in acknowledgement.

"Two-Tongues, your name was Tony; your grandma named you. And Smoothman, your name is really Simon, true?"

Both of those men looked at her, nodding, more than impressed.

"Byends, your name was Ben, and your parents loved you—a lot. You were even baptized as a child, remember?"

Then she held their hands, one at a time, to show acceptance. "Ben, Tony, Frank, Winston, Simon: believe me! God wants more for you than this!" she exhorted. Her voice was stirring and sure.

By that time, Byends had pulled over, just two-tenths of a mile from the Faire. The thugs were melting. Their hard, calloused hearts were actually *melting*. They were reliving fragments of memories of when someone had loved them, had shown them the love of Christ. Hope was searching deeply in their eyes now, imagining them before Apollyon had gotten his hooks into them.

"Chris and me, we want you to come with us to the King. . . . How 'bout it, friends?" she asked, her voice the essence of honesty and sweetness.

"Aw, hell," broke out Byends. "We'll go. We'll go, but, if Apollyon finds us, he'll kill us. Yas better not let us down. I did pick yas up the first time, afore I knew 'xactly who yas was, 'member that. . ."

"Dear brother, you can trust us," said Hope.

Christian was dumbfounded at this turn of events.

"It comes from God, Christian, from God," she whispered to her friend.

* * *

So, they drove to where Christian thought he could make out the right way again. It picked up from the mall and was marked "Salvation Road," luckily. But it was closed to traffic, a great barrier set up in front of it. "Follow me," Christian said.

They ran to a poorly maintained, concrete sidewalk inside the familiar, high walls. The path was beginning to go up again. When Christian saw a large slope coming into view, he knew they'd be in for another difficult time.

The pilgrims and the henchmen were soon all walking in step, just beginning to feel almost comfortable with one another. They could smell fresh, salty air and felt a slightly humid, though not unpleasant, breeze.

Fasinbothways suddenly felt a vibration in his pocket. He took out his pager and read a summons from Apollyon. He showed it to Hope and Christian. Everyone stopped. Christian was stressed, remembering the recent assault he had had with the monster.

Hope made the first move. "Listen, we haven't got much time. Your boss will know something's wrong soon. We've got to get way away from Vanity Faire, and now!"

"Even if we run, Apollyon kin fly faster," Byends objected. "He kin find us-- he kin *smell* us."

"He's right," said Christian. "Now, I'm not saying he'll be able to kill us, because he's been wounded pretty bad, but I agree-- he would if he could. If he does, we've got to make sure we'll all meet up afterwards. . . So, men," Christian said assertively, "you're going to have to say the Sinner's Prayer with us. You have to believe in your hearts that the King is your savior. And you have to confess it!"

The five former servants of Apollyon looked confused, but they went along with Christian's wishes.

"Come on, guys; just up here, I think there's a place we can do it," Christian said eagerly. When they got to the area, a scenic overlook of Vanity Bay, Hope and Christian gently pressed on the men's shoulders, directing them to kneel. Hope began to say the prayer, and all five recited line by line after her.

She was nearing the end of it, anticipating how she'd soon be leading her new converts toward freedom.

But something awful was happening instead. Christian immediately saw that the five now had gigantic packs on their backs, far bigger than Christian's had ever been. The masses were in fact heavier than a person, hundreds of pounds each. The men screamed in anger, in horror. Their knees gave way, and they went falling to the ground. They tore uselessly at the backpacks.

Then they turned on Hope. "You did this! Yer a witch!"

All the while, Christian was trying to talk over them, explaining that these terrible weights were the accumulation of all their past sins, and that it was OK, because the men had taken the first step in being made clean. "We'll go to the cross! We'll go to the cross!" he shouted, trying to calm them down.

But it was pointless. The five were overwhelmed with fear, not understanding. Or perhaps they understood but were unable to believe that anything could legitimately expunge their manifold offenses. As they tore at the straps of each other's burdens, trying to assist each other in their removal, their fingers lit up in flames, nullifying their frantic efforts. They let out shrieks of unadulterated fright.

"Please! Please!" shouted Christian. "I had one too! The King will take them if you bring them to Him!" But again, what he said fell on deaf ears. Too much honesty. Too much truth. Too much responsibility.

It was in that next, unspeakable moment that Byends, the henchmen's long-time leader, stepped over the guardrail. He threw himself over the colossal, jagged cliff, onto the unforgiving boulders of the seashore below.

Christian and Hope could not bring themselves to look over the edge, and their main concern then was for the others. But, sadly to say, the others had always been followers, not leaders. In their foolish rashness, Two-Tongues, Whateva, Fasinbothways, and Smoothman were quick to follow Byends. Horrible outcries were released as each plummeted to his untimely doom.

Then, there was the thunderous silence of nothingness, not even a wave daring to break.

Chp. 29 "The Grass is Never Greener"

"The fear of the Lord is the beginning of wisdom."
[Proverbs 9:10]

On that high slope of Salvation Road, Christian and Hope broke down. "I was so close!" Hope cried to Christian, imploring him for comfort.

He hugged her. "There, there, sweet girl. You did

your best. It was up to *them*. . . And don't forget," he added, "—you saved *me*." But he was only faking strength for her.

Hope brushed away tears that still would not fall.

The two continued walking on the road. From time to time, they could see brief glimpses of another, lower road running parallel to their own. When Christian began to feel better, he broached some conversation.

"How did you do that? --Know their real names, I mean," asked Christian. "Are you psychic or something?"

"No," answered Hope. "I merely looked into them as the King does. I treated them as if they were already the people I knew they could be once again."

Christian smiled to show his comprehension.

"That's a beautiful thought," he said. "I don't know if it could have ever really worked, though—I mean, about the future."

"You *don't* know, Christian," she said. "But God does. He sees everything that will ever happen in our entire lifetime; all our ups and downs: God sees them before we ever do."

The seaside road wound its way down and around, coming closer to the bay. Neither Hope nor Christian worried about of the possibility of Apollyon finding them. They just kept on keeping on.

At one point, Christian wanted to look backwards, to see if he could see the great flags and banners from the mall rooftop.

"No," Hope cautioned, before Christian could turn. She knew what he was considering. "I have a bad feeling about it. Don't do it," she ordered.

Sometime hours later, near nightfall, Christian and Hope found an old, gray-white statue near the shore. Its form was chiseled in lines of defiant grandeur. The eyes had no irises or pupils, giving it a scary look. It was turning at the waist, peering around, an incipient expression of horror at the corners of its lips.

Hope licked her finger, rubbed it against the statue, and then licked the finger again.

"What are you doing?" asked Christian.

"Tasting for salt," she said.

"But it's too perfect to have been created by the sea," Chris protested.

Knowing scripture inside and out, Hope concluded that it was Lot's wife, from Sodom and Gomorrah in the Good Book, whom God had turned to salt. "She wasn't supposed to look back, Chris," said Hope. "And neither should we. That's His way of telling us," she said, prophetically.

*　　*　　*

Christian and Hope traveled onward, away from the sea, taking never more than a catnap here and there, and rarely slowing. They walked along a river, an outlet of the bay, for many days and nights. Sometimes Christian leaned on Hope, and sometimes Hope leaned on Christian. They continued on in this way until the lack of sleep finally began to catch up with them. It was affecting their thinking. Food was the furthest thing from their mind, and both were beginning to have double vision.

One evening, they became uncharacteristically impatient with both each other and the process of getting there and seriously began to consider going over the wall, onto the other road.

"I've seen that road the entire time we've been on this one," observed Hope. "It's never anywhere else but right beside us. It's smoother, with far fewer kinks. The grass is greener by it, too. We could save time that way, and wear and tear on our bodies. I say we go," she propositioned.

"I see your points," Christian offered, "and we should be fine." He wanted to please Hope. Too bad for them both that she hadn't ever known Faith and had trouble sticking to the King's rules at times.

They could visualize themselves and what it would be like when they fell over onto the easy path of the alternate road. In their minds' eyes, they landed in each other's arms and laughed with delight.

Why didn't we think of this before? Christian asked himself, reviling his former reserve.

And so, without further ado, both Hope and Christian jumped the wall.

Chp. 30 **"Derailed"**
"The proud helpers fall under the slain." [Isaiah 10:4]

The grass was in fact greener over there. The road was indeed smoother, with fewer twists. The river was lovely. Also, the walled road remained safely in sight for the time they would have to take it up again.

The pair walked along renewed, a spring in their step. They felt exhilarated, living on pure adrenaline.

* * *

That morning, they met a fellow named Vane Confidenz, who attested that he was headed for the Celestial City. Christian and Hope immediately hit it off with Vane, who seemed so decent, so together, so "with it." He was outgoing and ultra positive, and in that way, seemed much like Gabby, minus the obnoxious banter. He was walking along the picturesque road with a lot of determination and confidence, and uplifting, *regular* things to say.

"How long have you been traveling this road?" asked Christian.

"Oh, not long," answered Vane. "I'll be there soon."

Vane looked excellent, no worse for the wear. He wore a wrinkle-free, white jacket, and there wasn't a dirt or blood mark on him.

"Did you go up two mountains and down two valleys?" asked Christian.

"No, can't say as I did," said Vane.

Wow, thought Christian, *this guy works smart, not hard. He did it better than we did.*

"Looks like you two been through some rough times," Vane noted, semi-sympathetically, with a hint of superiority.

"Oh, ya, that other road over there, over the wall, it's really rough. I won't go into it now, but needless to say, we're glad to have found a new way," said Christian.

Vane's steps were slightly ahead of Hope and Christian's. Before long, Vane's bearing was beginning to gnaw at Christian's self-esteem. *How can he have so much energy and luck? He's so much better than me.* Christian was ruminating, using toxic comparisons that his Father in Heaven never would have.

Playing off Christian's inferiority, Vane kept prodding them to talk about their prior mistakes.

And, although Christian was reluctant to talk about them, he yielded to the pressure. "We never really had a plan or a map, and I lost my Bible earlier on," said Christian, lowering his head.

Vane was eating this up.

"If I had to do it over again, I would do it all differently. Next time, I'd avoid all the hassles. I mean. . . we even had the Prince of this land, a real nasty character, hunting us down. That's who I got most of these marks from. Thank goodness there's been no sign of him here." He looked up and over to Vane like a big brother.

"Don't beat yourself up, kid. You've got me now. I'm a winner; I'll teach you how to have confidence in yourself!—how to keep your train on the track!" asserted Vane, holding his head high. He was quickly becoming their idol. He was good, and he was smart. He believed in himself and in them.

The hours rolled over into the early afternoon. Vane, the leader, began to walk more rapidly, and he was getting farther and farther ahead. Periodically, he'd stop and call to his new friends to hurry and catch up, and they would. Vane would pat their heads.

One of those times while Vane was waiting, he pulled out a pocket mirror and checked his face. He looked at the flawless texture of his skin, the graceful lines of his slim nose. His deep, dark blue eyes were entrancing, and he knew it. He closed the mirror with a snap.

"So friends, how ya doin'? Seems like you need an energy boost. Are you sure you want to go with me? I mean, if my pace is too fast, you might feel more comfortable taking it a bit slower. Think about it, OK, and let me know."

"Oh, no, sorry," answered Hope. "We want to stay up with you, because the sooner we get there, the better. We'll try to go a little faster, right Chris?"

"Absolutely," said Christian, weary.

* * *

After a few more interchanges, it was obvious that it wasn't working out. "Hey guys," said Vane, "I'm just gonna go on ahead for awhile. You don't mind, right? That way I can sort of be your lookout, you know. I can let you know what's coming." His real intention, of course, was to ditch them as soon as possible.

Hope and Christian shook their heads OK; what else were they going to say? Vane walked on, whistling a little tune as he went.

Vane did keep his promise and turn around a few times. "Wait till you see this, guys!" he yelled. "A beautiful field of dandelions, far off in the distance!. . . They're such pretty flowers, and so fast-growing too! I bet they just popped up overnight!" His silhouette stood at the crest of a small hill, illuminated by the strong rays of the afternoon sun.

But as Vane went to turn back around and proceed, he lost his footing. Because he never, ever made it his habit to look down, he couldn't see that the land immediately in front of him had given way. It was a blind cliff. Vane was falling into a deep pit engineered by Satan to catch fools. It indeed caught him so off guard that he never made a sound.

Christian and Hope turned to each other in panic. "Where did he go?" Christian sputtered.

"I have no idea! Let's go see!" returned Hope.

So they both cautiously ran up the small rise. And although it was a bit of a shock to find the land end so abruptly, they did perceive it before it was too late. They peered carefully over the edge, holding each others' arms protectively.

"Oh dear God!" cried Hope.

A huge sigh escaped from Christian's lungs.

At the bottom of the cliff, perhaps fifteen stories high, in an ashy, gray pit, lay the body of Vane Confidenz, splattered beyond all recognition.

* * *

Caught up in the drama of Vane's demise, neither Christian nor Hope realized that their fair road had departed from the walled one. They were bewildered about why the King would have let Vane die.

"He had so much belief in himself, and he had such great ideas for the future. . . You know, though, come to think about it," said Hope, "he never once mentioned the King. Maybe he didn't even care about him."

"Maybe," said Christian, mindlessly. "We've got to think of the best way down this cliff."

"Wait," Hope interjected, "why do we even have to? We should just go back onto the first road, the one with the walls. Even though it was really hard, I bet it'd be better than trying to get down this thing. I mean, look at him. Do you really want to chance it?"

"You're right," returned Christian. "But where's the path?" he asked with an inner jolt, realizing they were lost.

"Oh, no!" lamented Hope. "I have no idea."

It was at that moment that Christian realized that he deserved none of the credit for anything they had done while on the first path. "The King's got to be our leader— all the time," he said to Hope.

"Yes, our confidence must rest in him, not in any person," Hope agreed.

So they went back over the area they had just covered, attempting to locate the point at which the two roads had diverged. But a rainstorm was beginning, and the once placid river was rising.

It became an indomitable monster within minutes. Floodwaters raged and spilled over its banks. Before they even knew it, Christian and Hope had been swept away.

Chp. 31 "Going Nowhere Fast"

"My soul chooseth strangling rather than life." [Job 7:15]

The two rebels were buffeted mercilessly by the tremendous force of the current. It catapulted them along, dashing their bodies against rocks. When they could come up for air, they'd scream for each other, but Mother Nature was beyond their puny powers. Thrown, thrown, thrown they were, somersaulting over and over. Time hammered itself out to a narrow thread of fear, like it does when we feel as if we're about to die accidentally.

After what seemed like an eternity, the two were spit out of the furious gush and deposited on the grounds of a huge structure. It was a dull, gray fortress of some sort, with high, gothic turrets and sharp-angled gables. They saw it while lying on their backs.

"I doubt we're going to be able to find the walled road now," moaned Christian miserably, eyes closing.

"I doubt it too, Christian," said Hope, for the first time in her life a pessimist. Her voice was weak from fainting. Total exhaustion now replaced the false exhilaration they had felt only hours before. They heard the drip, drip, drip of their waterlogged clothes onto the dirt where they had landed. Under shut eyelids, their bodies were still feeling the sensation of being tossed.

*   *   *

Suddenly, a booming bass voice startled them back to reality. "Wake up!"

Christian opened his eyes to see innumerable gargantuan keys suspended from a blinding, metal key ring. Looming above them was the producer of the sound, the possessor of the keys-- an incredibly huge giant. His sight was focused like a laser beam onto Christian. His foot was stepping on Christian's pant leg. *Caught like drowned rats*, Christian thought.

The giant spoke slowly, each syllable shaking the ground like a bomb. "Welcome to Dowting Castle, my home," he said, his breath repulsive. "You're going nowhere else."

Precisely then, his firm stance unraveled and he began to shake. His erratic tremors were terrifying. *Will he fall on me?* Hope worried, praying that she wouldn't be crushed to death by this foul-smelling fiend.

Then, the tremors stopped, and the giant just stared into space for a moment. When he came to, he picked up on the conversation as if nothing had happened.

"My name is Despo. Be thankful I am rescuing you," he said, picking up each of their pant legs with a tiny pinch of bulbous fingers. The giant carried them upside down, swinging in the air, to his dwelling.

When they were inside the fifty-foot door, the epileptic giant took them down a monumental staircase. The staircase stopped at the cellar. The captives' nostrils and lungs were immediately permeated with the most vile stench imaginable, like that of decomposing flesh. Christian and Hope gagged repeatedly.

The giant stood over a large, grim trash compacter and released his hold. Their heads hit the bottom with a thud, nothing there to cushion them. At least they had somehow missed the blades.

The giant put something on top of the hole, then left, locking the cellar door.

"Oh, how awful!" Hope yelled. "That smell! It stinks worse than anything!"

In the spotty light, Christian checked his certificate. It was drenched from the flood, so he had to unfold it carefully. The ink had smeared badly, the paper disintegrated at some folds. Luckily, though, his name was still visible. He pressed the wrinkles and warps out as best as he could and laid it out to dry.

After a few hours of containment, the odor did not bother them as much anymore. The two began to talk over plans of escape, but it was hard for Hope to think.

Christian tried to climb up through the opening of the trash compacter, but a load of heavy garbage prevented him like a stubborn lid.

Christian brainstormed every possibility, but nothing seemed plausible, or survivable. "Even if we could somehow get out of this thing, he locked us in the room." *If I could only get out and nab his key!*

The moonlight coming in through the cellar window mocked them. They so desperately wanted freedom.

* * *

Two nights and two days went by without food, without water. The hunger pangs obsessed them.

The metal of the compacter conducted heat and cold readily, and the temperature extremes were brutal. When it rained outside, they shivered. When the sun beat through the cellar window, it felt like a microwave oven.

And Hope must have sustained quite a head injury in the flood-- *probably a concussion,* Christian thought-- because there were long periods in which she was out.

Beyond these physical problems was the morbid sense of failure. Mulling over the dismal situation, Christian became worse than depressed. He cursed the day he was born. He was disheartened, desperate, and basically alone. He was without a god, abandoned. Another night came and wasted away.

* * *

On the morning of the third day, the giant Despo entered the dungeon and took each teen out for some sport. He beat them to a bloody pulp with one of his massive tire irons.

He stood back for a few moments, rubbing his chin. He had brought them to the brink of death, but no more. He finished pondering his handiwork, then replaced them in the dirty appliance.

"That oughta fix ya," he bellowed. The wind from his putrid breath felt like a hurricane. "And if not, there's always suicide."

The giant brushed over the layer of refuse, then suddenly began to shake, succumbing to another one of his fits.

After he came to, he left again, his keys jangling into oblivion.

Chp. 32 **"The Key"**

"He that wandereth out of the way of understanding shall remain in the congregation of the dead." [Proverbs 21:16]

By that night, both Christian and Hope, having been left to rot, were so dehydrated that it was clear they could no longer endure. "So thirsty, so sore," groaned Hope. "I think I'm dying," she whimpered, barely clinging to life.

I wish he would just come in and kill us, but he won't, thought Christian. Flashes of his life's darkest experiences came in and out: the scene of his dad leaving the family, the time when his dog was killed. Even if he could have helped himself, it was far too much effort. Better to help death come. *Then all the worry, pain, and sadness in my life will be done with, forever.*

These were going to be his last words, for Christian had decided to kill himself.

But to leave her in misery wouldn't be fair. . .

His thoughts warred. Despairing, Christian thought, *Her suffering could continue for who knows how much longer. Anything but to go on as we are, in limbo.* There had to be an end to this and now. . .

He didn't even have the strength to sob. In his heart, he had decided to finish it for her, then deal with himself. *But how?* His gun was gone, probably taken by Despo when he lay half unconscious in front of the castle.

The shiny, sharp steel of the machine's blades called: *slit her wrists!* Christian heaved Hope over his shoulder, wishing he could turn back time.

* * *

Just then, Christian heard the rattle of the key in the cellar door. Their captor was returning. He swore when he saw they were still alive. "Why won't you die?!" he yelled, infuriated at their hardiness.

"*Do* us, why don't you?!" Christian said defiantly, no longer scared.

"I don't kill anybody; they kill themselves," said the giant, low and raspy. And although Christian could not see any bodies, he knew it was true-- from the noxious atmosphere that infiltrated everything.

"We want to die, but there's no way to do it," Christian lied, hoping he could bring just a little inconvenience into Despo's life. "What can we use to take our own lives?"

The giant reached into his pocket, the size of a tent, and pulled out Christian's tiny gun. He threw it down the compacter.

Christian picked up the weapon, turning it over, contemplating. Hope was awake now, resting on her knees, crying, motioning with her hand to bring on the bullet. Christian lifted the weapon, aiming it at Hope, shaking. The giant listened in heightened anticipation, enjoying their torment.

I'm about to commit murder, a tiny voice said in Christian's mind, almost not perceptible. Christian hesitated, then aimed at the bottom of the compacter and shot.

Frustrated, Despo yelled, even louder this time. "Why won't you do it? ... Do it! Do it!"

Suddenly, the giant was seizing again. He slowly collapsed, his hand grabbing onto the compacter, inadvertently flipping the switch.

* * *

The compacter's blades began to turn. Christian shoved Hope into a corner, then ran to another. The blades spun on the shaft in a blur, cutting the air, but not them.

But then rushing water came, running down the drain and loosening their hold. It wouldn't be long before they were diced and disposed of as common garbage.

Dear King, Christian begged, *please help us in our hour of need!*

The saying *God doesn't make junk* popped into his mind right then. The machine began to smoke, then came grinding to a halt. In an act of God, the bullet had somehow worked loose and then lodged between gears.

With the giant incapacitated, perhaps there's a way to escape, thought Christian. He climbed up easily through the hole, up into the basin. But Despo wasn't a heap on the floor as Christian expected. Fortuitously, the sink had caught him by the crook of the arm, and he lay dangling there.

"Please, Hope, try to stand up. Come to the hole, and take my hands." Christian hollered this, knowing that if he could just get her up there, they'd be able to use the giant's arm as a bridge. He prayed for the King's power to strengthen her.

Miraculously, she was there, stretching up her arms. Christian grabbed hold and pulled her up. He lifted her into his arms.

It was grueling, but he managed to carry her up Despo's forearm, then turn at his elbow and go down his upper arm and back. The giant didn't even flinch. And when they came to the cellar door, it was open!

127

It was time to tackle the staircase. Christian lifted Hope's body onto the first step, then jumped up to where she was at. He did this step by step, repetitiously.

He thought they were home-free until he checked the front door. It was locked; Christian wanted to once again fall apart.

The key was still fastened securely to the ring on the giant's belt. Going back to take his key was out of the question; it might take too long, and would certainly wake him. Shimmying under the door was impossible too, as even their emaciated bodies were too big for the slit.

King, tell me; there's got to be a way! prayed Christian. *Please!* he repeated. His mind was reeling, as it had so many times before.

Then he became indignant. *King, you promised me! I claim power in Your Name!* A strange surge of energy zapped through the atmosphere.

That's the key! said Hope, fully reviving. Christian recalled Evan's words: "Knock, and it shall be opened."

So Christian simply knocked on the door, knowing it would somehow give way as it had at Loveland's gate, way back on the very first day of his journey. And, in accordance with his complete belief, the castle door sprang open.

Christian fled the castle with Hope, out into the inhospitable darkness.

* * *

They ran for their lives, back through where the flood had ravished the land, until they came to the place the following evening where they had so foolishly gone off the King's road. They climbed back over to safety and went to sleep cradling the wall.

Christian and Hope were determined that no one else should make such a detour and, the next morning, took time to make a sign, using debris from the flood. They pounded it down into the sod, securely, and went on.

Part 4: The Passage

Chp. 33 "Lead Us Not Into Temptation, But Deliver Us From Evil"

"By the word of thy lips I have kept me from the paths of the destroyer." [Psalms 17:4]

Not far down the road between the concrete walls, the sides gradually diminished in height, so that before long, there were no more walls at all. This concerned Christian and Hope, who, after learning their lesson, had come to prefer them for the stability and certainty they provided.

It was on that wall-less road that Christian and Hope encountered three shepherds standing there silently, tending their flocks in the warm sunshine. All three had shepherds' crooks, but each was dressed in a different kind of robe. There was something different about them, but neither Hope nor Christian could exactly place their finger on it.

"Why, hello, my children," said one of them, calmly, assuredly. He was wearing a fine, blue robe, with a white sash around his neck. "I see you are traveling the road to the Celestial City. How has your journey been so far?"

Christian and Hope were too shy and self-concious to answer, feeling as though they could have avoided their last mishap had they only stayed on the right road.

"Hmm," said the same shepherd, "in that case, allow me to introduce myself. I am Knowledge. My friends here are Experience and Sincerity. We live on this land, shepherding the King's flock. We'd like to offer you His assistance."

"Thank you, but we don't need your help," answered Christian with perverse boldness. "We've been through a lot already and made it OK. Besides, this part looks rather easy."

"That's good to hear, my child," said Experience, a little skeptically. He was the one wearing the dull brown robe, threadbare and filled with patches. *He looks just about as bad as me,* thought Christian.

Christian furrowed his eyebrows, thinking about the shepherd's names. "Your names. . . we've never heard of anyone with names like those. . . of *qualities* like that. Beg my pardon, but how did you get them?" A myriad of feelings besides curiosity were rising up in Christian, like bravado, and even resentment. *What gives him the right to have a name like Knowledge? Nobody knows everything!*

"The King, actually, bestowed them upon us," said Knowledge.

"Each of us began our earthly lives lacking these very traits," explained Experience.

"Our lives were about first learning how to accept the need for them--" said Sincerity, the one with the spotlessly clean white robe like Christian had once possessed.

"--And then growing to possess them," finished Experience. "Once we achieved them," he continued, "our earthly missions were complete--"

"--And the Lord now enables us to remember those times—" elaborated Knowledge.

"--And the importance of our journeys with those names," finished Sincerity. "Now, we are here to speak to certain passersby, the ones who need us," said all three, in remarkable unison.

"You see, then, although you *say* you do not need

us, we know there is no mistake," offered Sincerity. "You *do*."

Christian's face looked mortified as he recognized his foolish pride. "You're right. I wasn't being sincere. I have relatively little experience, and I still don't have all the knowledge I need to have to make it through this life. I know *that*, at least." He took in a big breath of air and sighed.

"Oh, good," said Sincerity, hugging Christian. "We can work with that."

They all turned and walked, the shepherds taking up their staffs.

"Does what you said mean that you've already been to the Celestial City?" asked Christian.

"Yes," said Experience. "We have."

"Then you are dead," said Christian.

"Oh, no," interjected Hope. "I think they are *angels*."

Knowledge, Experience, and Sincerity smiled a little. They did not answer. They only got down to their assignment.

*   *   *

They began to steer the young adults through the spectacular Delectable Mountains, which they acknowledged were truly gorgeous, but warned would be filled with varied experiences and temptations. "Something like life," said Experience, giving a little nod of the head, reminiscent.

The mountains in the late springtime were majestic purple and blue, with white caps of snow and wildflowers everywhere. Becks came to stand in fresh pools of water as if to quench Hope and Christian's thirst on command. They knelt beside the small streams, drinking and splashing each other, happy and protected.

Christian and Hope trekked onward with Knowledge, Experience, and Sincerity, their friendly guides. The angels showed the two where to find honey and berries. There were nuts and seeds of all kinds. There were vineyards so full of grapes, red, green and purple, that Christian and Hope could gorge themselves as much as they liked. Memories of gnawing hunger vanished. The Delectable Mountains were a little piece of Paradise on earth.

That wasn't to last forever, though. The angels knew what was coming. True to their words, there was as much danger as beauty in these hills.

* * *

The shepherds showed the two young pilgrims a cliff called Arror, where people were lined up to go sky diving. "Oh, I've always wanted to do that!" cried Hope, too excited.

"No," said Sincerity.

Little did those foolhardy daredevils know, explained Experience, that their parachutes weren't real and would never open. The shepherds urged their charges to see the other side, the base of the overhang, where there were bodies dashed to pieces.

Christian remembered the tragic demise of Vane Confidenz. He thought of Mr. Hip, who had also fallen to his death. In addition, he could not help recalling Apollyon's henchmen who had followed Byends to their gruesome ends.

"Why so many fallen people?" Christian asked searchingly. There was no ready answer from the others, but a thought leapt into his mind.

"I know," he surmised. "It's because they acted rashly, carelessly, impatiently. They took risks that were too great—risks that required them to gamble on the things of this world. They were impetuous, not gauging the consequences."

Hope then wondered: if people saw examples of others coming to bad ends, why didn't they avoid such similar fates? Why were they doomed to repeat errors? The shepherds, preferring the two teens to work out their own answers, were quiet.

"I think I know. . . " said Hope in answer to her own question. "My mother used to say 'hindsight is twenty-twenty.' I think she meant that it's hard to see our own mistakes coming, and even if we have seen those of others, we never think they could happen to us."

The shepherds looked satisfied and continued on the path, leaning on their staffs with each step.

* * *

The shepherds brought Hope and Christian to another important area, called Caushen Plateau, where there was a brick maze for adventurers. There even was a ladder propped up to it, ready to let them in. Christian thought it all looked interesting, but Sincerity told him not to go.

Inside, explained Experience, there were blindfolded people slowly walking among what were really tombs in a mausoleum. The more lost they became, the more slowly they searched, hoping to eliminate their mistakes. Knowledge drew out an infrared device and showed the pair a real-time, aerial picture detected through satellite. The futile groping of the unsighted was disturbing to watch.

Christian thought of his poor mother and brother, and the lonely pedestrian he had run into on the street, trapped back in Deastrukshun.

"What does this mean?" he asked, upset and sad for them, wishing he had only done more.

Again, the angels were strangely silent, but Hope and Christian understood their method.

"I guess maybe it means that if we are too cautious, overly cautious I mean, so careful about not making any mistake, we won't take the risk of trusting Christ, or believing in him, or even fully living. Is that right, Knowledge?"

Knowledge shook his head in affirmation.

"Do you trust the King every day of your life?" asked Experience.

"Yes, I try to," answered Christian.

"And do you really believe that He will show you The Way even when you cannot see it with your own eyes?" asked Sincerity.

"Yes, we do. We do," answered both Christian and Hope.

"Very good then," said Knowledge, proud of his students.

"And I see," said the clever Hope," that Error and Caution are opposites, nevertheless, two sides of the same coin. Error is acting recklessly, wrongly, and Caution is being indecisive, too slow to act for the right. Either way, both are going to get you in trouble." Christian thought back to the wild directionlessness of the hyper Talkative, to the heavy obstinacy of the immovable Obi.

The mentors and their well-grounded pupils proceeded to the next place of instruction.

*   *   *

Amidst the idyllic setting of song birds and sunflowers, a large hill had a man-made, neon door in its side. "Let's investigate!" shouted Hope.

But the shepherds refused. "Stay back!" said Experience.

When shut, warned the shepherds, the door seeped out poisonous gases that were invisible, tasteless, and odorless, so if someone stood there too long, it would asphyxiate him or her. When unlatched, however, the door would fly open and belch out deadly fire and smoke. It was another entrance to Hell where certain people from the Bible had sealed their fate through—you guessed it— indecision or recklessness. If there had been any way, their shades would have come to the door personally, imploring Christian and Hope to read their Bibles and stay away!

Christian was surprised to see such a tempting, direct route to the underworld from the path of Salvation, and protested it. "But I went to Hell by a long, low, dark valley. I had plenty of time to realize what I was getting into."

"Oh, I assure you," said Knowledge, "There are many paths leading to everlasting damnation: some of them long roads, and some of them quick entries. Don't be naïve; recognize and avoid them at all costs. Be vigilant, my son."

Christian was afraid.

Chp. 34 **"Clear View"**
"Believe on the Lord Jesus Christ, and thou shalt be saved." [Acts 16:31]

The group traversed up still another grand, craggy mountain. Somehow, the hard work of climbing was made oh so much easier with company. This mountain was not going to be an intimidating precipice; instead, said the angels, the top was a place of clarity for all who traveled there.

It would be a challenge, yes, but it would be worth it, said Sincerity.

"It's my favorite of these mountains," said Experience.

"You'll be able to survey the vast expanse of God's creation and feel his omnipotence and artistry," said Knowledge.

Once they did get to the summit, Christian and Hope knew it was called Mt. Clear for a reason: there was never a cloud in the sky nearby. You could indeed see into the distance for miles.

Even more wondrous: Christian saw not only the walled path but all of the places he had ever been to on his journey, all the way back to Deastrukshun. The gate by the cornfield was a very small beam of light, intensely bright. The Valleys of Humiliation and the Shadow of Death looked like deep, dark ripples in the land's rich tapestry. The church and Vanity Faire were there, like tiny landmarks. The first hill, with the child's cross, was there too. Christian noted that all of the hard parts of his journey looked much smaller than they had seemed while he was experiencing them.

"So you have seen your problems from this higher stance," said Experience.

"Yes," said Christian, who now recognized he had made them so big in his head.

"This is the proper perspective," added Sincerity.

"This is the view that Experience gives you," said Knowledge.

Then, Knowledge withdrew something long and silvery from his robe. It was a telescope. He gave it to Christian, who examined it fervently. Experience then set it up, but in the direction opposite from where they had been looking. Christian wondered what the angels wanted him to see.

Hope looked into it first and saw a heavenly light shining far away. "It's marvelous, Christian!" she exclaimed.

"Ah, the gleam of the Celestial City," said Knowledge.

Christian could barely contain himself. Hope moved aside so that he could look.

Christian positioned his eye in front of the lens. For the first time in his life, he saw with his own eyes that the Celestial City was real, not a fairy tale.

"We wanted to give you a glimpse of your future," said Sincerity. "So you will know that the angels always believe in you. We know you are sincere."

"It's beautiful, really beautiful," remarked Christian. "If I look close, I can see not only white light, but little pieces of green, blue, yellow, and pink too."

"Yes," said Knowledge. "It is made of precious stones and fabulous jewels of all kinds: jade, onyx, turquoise, amethyst, pearl, emerald, ruby, to name a few. The streets are paved with gold."

"It's magnificent," commented Hope. "I can't wait to get there!"

"You don't have that long to go now," said Experience, "but we must leave you. We have done what we needed to do, and you must face the next part on your own."

Christian complained. "But can't you please just stay with us? We still need your help."

"No," said Experience. "You now have enough resources."

Christian protested again. "But each challenge is new! Nothing is ever the same!"

Experience addressed this with a steady voice. "My child, there is nothing new under the sun. Each challenge can be solved by living the Christian life. Apply the values of faith, hope, and love, and you will be lifted up in the end."

Christian saw the wisdom in the statement. "But angels," he said, "Could you possibly tell us what specific obstacles wait for us in the final stretch?"

"In particular," Sincerity said, "You will have to pass through 'The Enchanted Ground.' There, everything will seem magical, but do not let that seduce you. It isn't real. Stand firm in your beliefs."

"And," added Sincerity, "Beware of the Flatterer as well. He is not Sincere, though he will look it."

This is some important information, though not enough, thought Christian.

"Ah, my dear, dear boy, would it be any better," posed Knowledge, "if humans had crystal balls? Would it help you to know the future, to plan for things, or would it be more a source of anxiety, knowing what bad things are going to happen? Life is a test-- use all that we have given you, our Knowledge, Experience, and Sincerity."

"I will, thank you," answered Christian, understanding that there were some responsibilities, like living a life, that one had to do for himself. "But it's so painful at times, so miserable, so lonely. Why can't it just be over?!" He broke down in sobs.

All three angels converged on him and Hope, embracing them. Their warmth was so nurturing, their condolences so soothing.

"It will be over when you are ready," said Experience.

"The final obstacles will determine the amount of faith, hope, and love, or lack thereof, within the person who responds," said Knowledge.

"They will be hard, so very hard," said Sincerity, not wanting to sugar-coat, "but only at the time," she said, accepting Christian's human frailty.

Christian appreciated the honesty, yet voiced another doubt: "But we don't have the love you speak of, or our Faith anymore! She's dead!" He tried to grab hold of the angel's gown, but his fingers were grasping at thin air.

"The body is dead, but the spirit lives on," all three beings conveyed.

Christian felt toyed with, frustrated, insecure.

Then, abruptly, one angel's tone grew very stern and he warned: "Remember, till your final moment in the body, the Prince of this earth, Apollyon, is lying in wait for you to trip up. He is an opportunist, a shark who smells blood. He will be there, at the wrong place, the wrong time, to bite through your soft spot." Experience said this as if he had been through it a thousand times.

Then, the angels were gone, having vanished into thin, mountain air.

Christian and Hope stepped away from the telescope, grateful for the encouragement, but afraid for the future-- not knowing what would happen next, only knowing that it wasn't over yet.

Chp. 35 "Ignorance is Not Bliss"

"There is more hope of a fool than of him." [Proverbs 26:12]

Soon after the angels departed, Christian and Hope got down from Mt. Clear. It wasn't too long before they met up with a boy—a boy, or perhaps a phenomenon—with the curious name of Igor Notbliss. He had Christian tattoos all over his body, a Christian rock band T-shirt on, and a cross shaved into the back of his hair. Very cool.

He was humming a well-known Christian tune about loving your neighbor, but when he began to talk, it was all about him. It was easy to see that Igor believed he was a terrific Christian, just like old Mr. Hip. He said he was *very* religious. "I do everything: give to charity, tithe, volunteer at church, fast, and pray all day."

"You're lucky you met up with me," said Igor, pridefully. "Christians, we gotta stick together, eh?. . . Say, where you off to?"

"Oh, we're going to the Celestial City. It's in sight now. We're so excited!" Hope said.

"Well, don't you think you should be on your way to church instead?" asked Igor, raising an eyebrow.

"No. We haven't been to church in a while," Hope said with a twinge of guilt.

"Then you guys are in real trouble," said Igor, as if he had all the answers, just like Gabby. "I'll start praying for your souls ASAP. I want you to come with me. I'll take you to my church. That's where I'm going right now!"

"Really, it's not that we don't want to go to church or that we've never been," explained Hope. "It's just that we were put on this course and have to finish it. We were told not to go off the path."

"Who told you that? Regular church attendance is imperative," Igor said pompously. "Don't you know that the King has a little book in heaven where he counts you in or not? Then, when you're dead, he adds it all up. If you were there almost every Sunday, with the exceptions of when you were really sick, of course, then he lets you in. If you weren't, and you skipped a lot, you're out, O – U – T, out, I say!"

"Hmm," said Hope. Igor's thinking didn't really line up with the voice inside of her, the one that came through her talks with God.

"So are you gonna come with me, or what?" Igor asked.

"No; we already told you our plans, but thanks," offered Christian, huffing and puffing to keep up.

"Fine; my way on this road ends here; the church is about a mile that-a-way." Igor pointed off to the left. "But we can talk for a minute. . . . You should know that I am an important, up-and-coming guy. I have a friend named Gabby, and me 'n' him, well, we're gonna set up our own church and get lots of people. Not just any church; I'm talkin' a *super*-church. The building's gonna be gi-normous! We're gonna have millions, maybe even zillions of members, and then get into broadcasting, with corporate sponsors. It's gonna make a name for itself, let me tell you. . ."

"So don't come cryin' back to me when we've got a famous televangelist network and you two have nothing. Remember, I gave you the chance to be counted in."

Christian and Hope laughed a little to themselves when they thought of the name Gabby, probably the same one they knew, whom they last saw spinning in circles and talking to himself in a field.

"Say, Igor, you've told us about your building plans, now tell us about what's going on inside of *you*," said Christian.

Igor was completely silent, almost as if the words were in some foreign language. After a while, Igor winged it and said, "What you're talkin' about--it don't much matter. What matters is bein' religious. I'm religious, and my daddy's religious, and his daddy's religious, and that daddy's daddy is religious too. Look here, I got sores on my knees from so much prayin', and everybody knows it." He bared his calluses.

"Bet you ain't got those," he continued. "Bet you ain't even been to church."

"He's ignorant of what it means to be real," whispered Christian to Hope, aside.

There was unease in the air. Hope and Christian were glad when Igor wanted to leave.

* * *

Then, suddenly, Christian, Hope, and Igor saw

seven devils coming along the road towards them, wearing red shirts embroidered with the Apollyon logo (a barbed, scarlet letter "A") and carrying a man bound and gagged. The man was squirming and trying to scream.

"Why, hello!" said Igor without batting an eyelash. Apparently he couldn't see their red garb, pitchforks, horns, or pointed tails.

"Hello," said one of the devils, slyly.

"And where are you going today? To church, I hope," said Igor.

"Yes, as a matter of fact," the devil responded, "but not until we have brought this man, Mr. Turnaway, back to the door of Hell." Christian and Hope knew he was referring to the entrance the angels had recently shown them.

"Back to the door of Hell?" asked Igor, concerned. "Didn't he go to church?"

"Oh, yes, he went to church every Sunday," said the devil, trying to limit the man's flailing.

"Then release him, I say! I command you to release him!" Igor yelled with fake authority.

"Oh, no, sir," said the devil, mincing no words. "His contract says 'To Hell.' He's sold his soul to the Devil, so that's where he goes."

"But there must be some mistake!" yelled Igor, growing increasingly irate.

"No mistake," said another of the devils, cavalierly.

"Just tell me how someone could go to church religiously and still be sent to Hell!" screamed Igor.

"Listen, Mr.," said the first devil, "We don't know the reason. We just carry out the order. All we can tell you is this: Turnaway told us he knew some old guys named Formalist and Heipokracy. He said he saw how bad they really were, and it turned him off from believing. 'Disillusioned,' is the word he used." The devil scoffed and added, "Really dropped his noble ideals, too, he said, after his niece, somebody named Faith, was murdered."

Igor listened to the shocking story while Christian and Hope felt the crushing weight of diabolical coincidence.

"Now that better satisfy ya, because we got work to do!" The devils were impatient. They marched away, and Igor soon shrugged off the incident. He went back to his former manufactured bliss, while Christian dwelled on the meaning of the incident for some time.

*　*　*

"Don't you see, Igor?" asked an impassioned Christian. "The King set that up so that you'd learn a lesson. Do you want to be like Formalist and Heipokracy and sabotage people who need real religion?"

"Well, . . ." said Igor.

"Please, please come with us!" Hope implored.

Christian and Hope pulled on him, and he agreed to go, providing that he could turn back at any time. Igor walked along, going through the motions.

But Igor's heart wasn't in it; he was slow. Christian and Hope slowed for him numerous times, but it wasn't long before Igor was lagging far behind. It was drudgery, as Christian's grandfather had said, "like pulling teeth."

Eventually, all three of them came to an odd intersection, a complicated fork in the road. In fact, if you had been flying overhead in an airplane, it would have resembled the stem and five tines on a pitchfork.

"Go on without me; I'll catch up soon," yelled Igor to Christian and Hope.

"I'm worried about him," said Christian.

"Evidently, he has never met Sincerity!" said Hope.

Chp. 36 "Deception"

"A man that flattereth his neighbour spreadeth a net for his feet." [Proverbs 29:5]

Dusk was falling fast. Christian and Hope progressed down the walled path, the middle tine of the "pitchfork." Christian indicated to Hope to sit and rest for a bit, to let Igor catch up. "We need to be passionate, yes, but also patient with each other, Hope," he said, remembering a lesson he had learned from Interpretern. Hope agreed that they should wait.

Hope said, "Now, let's review what the angels told us, Christian. They said to apply our knowledge, experience, and sincerity, and, above all, to stay wary. We can do those things."

"You're right, Hope," said Christian.

The two pilgrims did not realize that Apollyon's energy was imminently approaching, a force like a black hole affecting anything and everything around it.

* * *

Igor caught up with them again. All three plodded along. Hours dragged on. There was something that felt foreboding, out of kilter. They noticed that the grass along the asphalt was brown, thin, patchy. The wall was in disrepair, but that was nothing new.

A shining white form was coming along the road with a rapid stride. It was glowing with fierce passion, almost hurting the eyes, as when you come out of a movie theater on a bright, sunny day, and have no sunglasses.

The mysterious presence came closer. Christian was shielding his eyes from the stupendous glare. There it was, a hooded robe before them. *This is obviously an angel of tremendous prowess*, thought Christian.

"My children," said the figure. "It is so wonderful to see you. I have just come from doing my Lord's work. He is so pleased that you are here. He was hoping we would meet."

Christian tried to look at the being's face, but it was impossible. The energy burned his eyes.

"It's a blessing to see young people as fine as yourselves on this trail. Most don't make it this far, you know," said the stranger, kindly.

"You know, my friends," said the figure, "you should congratulate yourselves. I have heard much about you and the things you have done. You are His Chosen."

This feels good, thought Christian.

"I assume that you are on your Way to the Celestial City, of course," said the being, "so please allow me to assist you."

Igor, Christian, and Hope were only too glad to have a guide again. *Surely the King expects to give us relief at some points,* reasoned Christian. The chill of the impending nighttime was vaguely unpleasant.

Then, with an unexpectedly sharp timbre, pointing down to the grass, the being said, "See how this ground is? It's not good enough for you. You deserve much better, my valiant heroes, spawn of the Most High. Come with me," he said, invitingly.

So the three young people and the nameless figure rashly went through a small aperture in the wall. The land was wooded. The three humans looked forward to the spirit being's promise of a better way. But the flora, disappointingly, showed no signs of being any healthier here.

They proceeded along, talking. This spirit was overflowing with praises for the youths, swathing them in accolades.

"You are so gallant," he said to Igor. "Your Lord will reward you with all the fame you desire shortly." Igor, of course, ate this right up.

And to Christian, he said, "You have been extremely strong. Your victory over Apollyon has been touted over all the country!"

The spirit also gushed with much flowery language for Hope, telling her she was the most lovely and quick-thinking soul he had met in a long time.

Christian looked at the trail, dim in the distance. The grass fifty feet ahead appeared green, the bright green of late springtime. Christian thought, *See, he is bringing us to where it's better.*

As the spirit launched into another eloquent discourse on all Igor's outstanding qualities, Christian kept his eye on that spot.

When they had reached it, the surrounding blades of grass transformed from fresh green to withered brown. Christian could have sworn that he also saw a supple, healthy leaf fall from a nearby tree, desiccating rapidly as it fell, landing in ashes.

Christian rubbed his eyes. Words formed in his head in disjointed fragments. *Very strange*, he thought, *but I won't mention it. This being is here to help us. . . I trust him. Perhaps we are all so holy now that the lesser things of earth cannot bear their lowliness against our supremacy, like he said. . .*

"Yes, give yourself a pat on the back, children. Remember your deeds. Your King doesn't see all that you do. He'll be expecting you to recount your greatness when you get there, you know."

Christian said to himself, *He's right. Once in a while it's good to 'toot your own horn,' like they say . . . Nobody else is gonna do it for you.*

Still, these new thoughts were something Christian wasn't used to, and he lowered his head in awkwardness and uncertainty. He was walking slightly behind the white-robed spirit now, and the terrain was clearly illuminated. *Why is he leaving charred footprints as he goes?* wondered Christian.

Something was wrong, terribly wrong. The path was covered in some kind of camouflaged, woven netting, its boxy lines too perfect to be part of nature.

Before the teenagers knew what had hit them, that net swooped upwards in a trap that, when seen by the King far above, looked like a nuclear bomb. Within, the teens were swinging from a rope lashed to a tall tree. The force of the unforeseen, violent motion had sent their shoes flying.

* * *

The being standing below them was laughing loudly, his shrillness hurting their ears. "You didn't think I had *meant* all that, did you?" he asked, not waiting for a reply. His degenerate laugher was ringing throughout the woods.

"My job here is done, so I must leave you poor, un*for*tunate souls. One of my colleagues will be along soon to co-*llect* you." He put great emphasis on certain syllables of words, as if to showcase his powerful speech.

The servant of evil quickly removed his glowing white robe and dropped it carelessly onto the ground, causing a nasty hissing sound, like oil on a scorching-hot frying pan. The hood gone, two gnarled horns stuck up into the air, the forehead exhibiting the blackened brand of his enslaver, the barbed letter A. His undergarment boasted narrow red and black swirling lines, each of them so intense as to make one's head spin, maybe even to draw the admirer into its vortex.

"Alas, you wanted to be so high, especially you, Igor, and now you are! . . ." The villain said this and stood there just a short moment, admiring his handiwork. Then, as if to leave a calling card, he hissed, "Beware the infamous Flatterer!" He gave a dramatic swing of the arm high into the air, followed by a sudden prostration of his whole body. He spit a venomous black glob onto the ground and, writhing, snake-like, slid away in it, his black and red coil pattern making his shape hard to follow.

Igor looked stupefied. Christian and Hope both turned to each other, thinking that they should have *known* better. "They even told us," said Christian.

"I know, I know," answered Hope, remembering Sincerity, feeling ill.

Chp. 37 "Repelled and Enchanted"
"Let thee and I go on knowing that we have belief of the truth, and no lie is of the truth." [I John 2:21]

Christian, Igor, and Hope were cramped together, contorted inside the snare.

"I can't believe I fell for his pack of lies," said Christian, dismayed.

"Nor can I," said Hope, disappointed in herself as well. Despite all their knowledge, experience, and sincerity, fighting the good fight posed innumerable difficulties. "Somehow, *doing* the right thing is usually much harder than *knowing* it."

From time to time, the net swung, if one of them made a sudden movement. The night fell quickly now, and with it came strange animal noises.

"We're somebody's supper," whined Igor.

"No, we're not," replied Hope. "Christian and I have been in a situation like this before. We'll be able to pray our way out of it."

So the three prayed throughout the moonless night. Prayers of sincerity, regret, and longing. Some prayers were audible; some not. Some were frantic; some controlled. Some were solo; some together. Some were tender, some cruel. Christ accepted all of them except Igor's insincerities.

The frail human trio clung to each other, trembling with fear in the cold night.

The morning came with little light.

Christian pressed his face against the prickly threads of the net, so that an impression formed on his skin. His energy was completely gone, and he stared into negative space.

* * *

Much later, Hope felt something fussing at the net-- not pulling exactly, but working at it nevertheless. Suspended in mid-air, an angel with dark, open wings was attempting to use a knife on the rope.

"No, no!" screamed Christian, confused. "Don't!"

Igor screamed back at Christian with hostility. "What do ya mean, 'don't'? It's trying to save us!"

"It could be another demon," yelled Christian. "It could be fake, just like the last."

The angel shook her head "no," wordlessly. She mouthed the word "Truth." She continued strenuously sawing at the rope with her dull blade. Soon, the threads split, and there was a hole big enough for one at a time to crawl through. The angel held each of them, one at a time, in her arms, beat her enormous, dark, feathered wings slowly, and gently laid them on the earth.

She pointed back to the road from which they had come. It was clear what she wanted them to do.

The angel followed the three. When Christian, Hope, and Igor reached the fated portal, they turned to thank the dark-winged angel. She closed her eyes, pressed her palms together with fingertips pointed up, and bowed her head, silently. Hope climbed back through the opening, then the two males did as well.

Christian, Hope, and Igor were soon firmly back on the proper way. It was day. The confines of the familiar, rugged walls comforted them.

* * *

Igor had once again fallen far, far behind, having second thoughts. But coming along from the opposite direction was a person wearing a suit and tie, who looked normal, even safe to talk to, maybe.

"Hello, my name's Christian, and my friend here is Hope," Christian began. Not wanting to come on too strong, though, Christian decided not to warn him about The Flatterer just yet.

"My name's A. Theist. Hope this weather clears soon," the man said perfunctorily, peering up into the featureless, dull sky.

"Me too," said Christian. *So he's identified himself. That's a good sign.* "What has you on this road today?"

"Just passing through," the man answered, digging his foot into the ground with a mixture of boredom and contempt.

"Well, that's nice," said Hope, enthusiastically. "We're on our way to the Celestial City, to see the King."

"Sorry; there's no King in this land," returned the man abrasively, looking down his nose at them as if they were lice.

"*Yes* there is; we've been told about Him by trusted sources," Christian replied.

The traveler criticized and rebuffed them, saying they had been sorrowfully misled to believe such a thing.

It was clear that the man was more than a little offended that they disagreed. "Jesus Christ!" he exclaimed in vain. "I've wandered this earth for years looking for such a king, and I know for a fact there isn't any! I have proof, real evidence. Just look at the ruination of our communities— by hurricanes, tornadoes . . .forest fires, droughts! Just look at the plagues, the warfare, the starving faces of millions! *Just look* at our own premeditated evil, so rampant in the world!!. . .And you tell me there's a King?!" His skin was steaming, his face scarlet with sarcasm. "What you believe in is mere myth," he added, with rattled intensity. "A pretty legend, that's all. Stop the daydreams and delusions."

Christian remembered the dark-winged angel who had mouthed "Truth" and he held his ground, respectfully. There was no reason to argue, except to save the man's soul. "Please listen to us," pleaded Christian. "If you continue to go that way, you're headed for death. We've seen it happen to many. Please come with us, where you will have eternal life!"

"Hmph! That's absurd!" A. Theist said with enmity beyond anger. It was more like a calculated jealousy that someone else could have the courage to actually believe against the tide of everything. It was as if underneath it all there was the most desperate need to deny others a king because he himself did not have one. "We're *all* headed for death! And I've got news for you. . . there's nothing beyond the Here and Now. When we die, we get put in a hole in the ground, where worms chew us up and turn us back into dirt—this dirt." He directed Christian's attention to the small patch of soil his foot had dug up. "That's it— that's the end. I'm sure of it."

"But I've seen the Holy Ghost with my own eyes! He's conquered death! Maybe the King himself isn't around here in the flesh, but he sees everything going on through his spirit and intervenes." Hope and Christian remonstrated with the man, not in indignation, but in confidence, telling him *they* had the proof. "We also know from The Good Book, from angels walking amongst us in the shapes of everyday people, from miracles of the unexplained--"

"No!" A. Theist interrupted forcefully, waving his arms. "That's fantasy. Like I said, we're born, we live, and we die. There's no heaven, no hell, no ghosts, no voodoo, just a brain shuttin' down. You don't still believe in the Tooth Fairy, do you?"

Christian and Hope shook their heads.

"So then I *caution* you! Stop wasting your time!" vociferated the self-assured man. "Go on with your lives and don't think about it. No one needs a king or a god to lead a good life anyway. There are plenty of people I know who are good, honest, decent people, and they are atheists as well. As a matter of fact, I'm going to meet up with a few of them at the Delectable Mountain Maze this afternoon, where we'll try to enjoy what little there is to in this life."

"But Mister, you can't go *there*! It's not what you think! Please, please, it will rot your soul!" Hope cried.

"I'll tell you once more," A. Theist went on, his controlled exterior crumbling, "drop your high-minded crusade. I'm a powerful man in this country, and if word gets back about you two harassing any more of my people around here, I'll have you *&!# arrested!" He said this, scurrilously, believing in something, at least-- the power of foul language.

The man straightened his rumpled suit jacket and proceeded away. "And even if there were a king, I'd be *&!# against him," he yelled in hindsight, his voice clashing with the hills in rancor.

* * *

Hope and Christian continued on their way. "You know," stated Christian, "A. Theist had some points. . . He talked about disasters; I was in the middle of an earthquake on the way here. He mentioned people starving; remember our time in Despo's dungeon? He said something about evil; that snake thing back there wasn't exactly good!

Everything he said is true, you know, Hope. I've been
labeled a criminal, cut up like a steak. The only thing that
hasn't touched me so far is disease. . ."

Hope nodded, patiently listening to her friend.
"And I pray it never does. . .But there is a purpose for
everything, don't forget. I wish I could tell you what the
purposes are, but I'm not skilled to understand. The King
will answer all of the questions you've ever had, when you
get there, dear Christian."

"Thank you, Hope," he said.

Christian was feeling low and wishing he could see
the angels again. He had no idea how long it would be now
until they reached the city, but he was tired of almost
everything on earth. And while there was no dungeon or
swamp here to explain it, he still felt a persistent, low-grade
moroseness that simply would not abate. Even in the
Delectable Mountains, the pavement was hard, the route
was lonely, and the walls were monotonous. They had to
hike on.

* * *

The following day, Christian and Hope came into a
new area, where the walls were very low again, and the air
was fresh and sweet. The sun shone down on them with
love, and the hills were laced with fruit trees. Christian and
Hope were doing well, except for the state of their bare
feet, which were beginning to bleed. Defying explanation,
soon the two each found new shoes along the road.

"See! The Good Lord does exist!" said Christian.

They tried them on, Christian helping Hope. His
heart beat faster as he touched her leg.

"I feel that we are getting closer," said Hope. "It
might be anytime now."

"Yeah," he responded, not knowing if she meant the
destination or their friendship.

Sometime late in that afternoon, after the two had
feasted on all the delicious fruit they could swallow, they

began to get sluggish. Christian and Hope both yawned.
Their eyelids grew heavy, as heavy as the thick aroma of
lilac trees that surrounded them, enveloped them. "Ah, the
Delectable Mountains," said Christian.

"I feel so lovely," said Hope, as if sauntering
through a pleasant dream. She and Christian agreed that
this was the nicest part of their journey so far. It was
enough to even make one want to stay.

"Let's rest, just for a little while, here," said
Christian to Hope, feeling full, safe, and content. He threw
his leg over the low, stone wall as if it were a heavy anchor.
Christian and Hope were both so very drowsy.

Hope joined him under the shade of a pretty lilac
tree. A soft and thick layer of pale lavendar petals served
as their bedding. Christian took off his shirt to relax in the
day's warmth. "It's so enchanting here," she said, as if she
had been overcome by some sweet spell.

Her words contained more than a feeling. They
contained geographical accuracy. Poor wayward and
gullible children; they had entered the forbidden ground
unknowingly.

Chp. 38 "To Persevere"
"There is none righteous, there is none that doeth good."
[Romans 3:10, 12]

Christian and Hope held hands. "Hope," began
Christian, a question floating through his smooth voice,
"What were you thinking when the Flatterer was telling us
all those good things about ourselves? Did you believe
him?"

Groggily, Hope answered, "Yes, Christian, though I
shouldn't have."

"But he was right, Hope. You *are* beautiful," he said, taking her softly in his arms.

"It's not about us, sweet Christian. It's God's grace that makes us who we are. . ." Her voice was trailing off.

Christian recognized what was happening, and he knew he couldn't hold out much longer.

Then, though he longed to kiss her, he suddenly lost his train of thought about Hope. There was something more important. . .

"Hope," said Christian.

"Huh?" yawned Hope.

". . .The angels. Didn't one say something about the Enchanted Place?"

Hope rolled over, murmuring, "Yes, Christian. Enchanted Place. . ."

"Hope, please listen!" Christian persevered, fighting to stay awake. "We've got to move on."

"Huh? So tired. . ."

"Hope! Hope!" Christian said, near her ear, shaking himself to alertness. "Wake up! Wake up! This is it, I know it!"

"Uh-huh," Hope sighed mindlessly, pressing for sleep. They had been walking for days, countless days, months perhaps.

"It's the Enchanted Ground Sincerity warned us about! You've got to get up! Please, Hope, please!" Christian shook her.

He roused himself and flung her over his shoulder, running with her, not looking where he was going. That wasn't important. They just had to get out.

Christian kept pumping his numb legs, sometimes losing his grip on her body. She was like a lead weight, an albatross around his neck. He shouted out to God for strength and for it to be over.

What was worse, though, was that nothing looked

the same. *We went only a few steps away from the wall. How can it be we're so lost?* As Christian ran, frightened, stumbling along in the ironically entrancing, warm sun, he thought he saw the mute, gray-winged angel, beckoning him to press on. Her gentle wings were flapping in slow motion, her kind smile encouraging.

But it was only a mirage.

Christian was overwrought with exhaustion. *I can't, I can't,* he said to himself, each step an ordeal. He fell, and there he was, on his knees, head to the ground, surrendering to sleep, to coma, to death, slumped over a lump of immovable flesh. It was the undeniable shutdown, like A. Theist had said.

The sun beamed down hotter, hotter, not so friendly now. Birds of carrion, vultures and crows, began to circle. Their instinct to feed was making them crazy, and they began to circle lower and lower. . . .

* * *

Rodney in his jail cell awakened with an awful start. His heart pounded in his mouth, his ears, his whole head. He was being attacked by panic so severe he was certain he was going to die. He was dripping with perspiration, ranting something, flailing his arms around violently. Had he been experiencing a dream? A nightmare?

Maybe, but not really. It seemed as if it had been some sort of initiation. . . a mandatory working out of something he needed to deal with, though what, he did not know. All he knew was that his life was full of lies; he had been a two-card in a poker game, and he didn't like it.

A guard flashed a beam of light onto the teen. "What's goin' on there, Middleton?"

But Rodney couldn't answer. His awakening was to prove very brief. He fell back under the iron arm of sleep before the guard could reach him. Incredibly, the same dream was pursuing him. . .

*   *   *

The Angel of Truth indeed found them again, a tiny dot on the face of the earth. She stood behind, wings enfolding them. The air inside grew cool. The magical perfume was not penetrating. Christian got jarred back. The pair was awakening from sleep, the kind from which one does not usually awake.

The angel took her finger and began to lovingly trace letters on Christian's back. She gently scrawled a P, then an E, then an R, S, E, V, E, R, and finally an E. Then she drew her dark wings back, and Christian and Hope were alive and alert.

"Time," the angel mouthed.

"We have so little 'time'!" Hope interpreted. "We have to get back over the wall before her protection wears off."

Hope and Christian held their breath, got up, and ran. When they finally had to breathe, they noticed that the thick atmosphere had dissipated for them only somewhat.

"It *is* the Enchanted Ground, Christian!" said Hope.

"Like they told us," said Christian.

"Like they told us," said Hope.

The angel observed them with a maternal glance, high in the sky. She was gone before the teens could say thanks.

"How best to stay awake now?" asked Christian.

"I say we talk through it," suggested Hope.

"Good idea," her partner said.

And it *was* a good idea. Some of the topics they reviewed then were ways to know right from wrong, and the ways we are to avoid doing wrong with the application of Christian values. They both agreed that of faith, hope, and love, love was the greatest. They talked of their fondest memories, their most meaningful experiences.

Christian told Hope about the House of the Holy, the church he had slept in so peacefully, pampered in loving care, recalling it in the most appreciative way. Hope spoke about her little life crises growing up and how her mother had shown her loving support. "My mother used to tell me that people are like rubber bands. 'God will never stretch you till you snap,' she said. 'He knows just how much to stretch you.'"

The things Christian and Hope were sharing were building a sense of special intimacy, not one based on hormones. The false niceties of the spell Apollyon had set upon this territory were cracking with every word. Something stirred in Christian. The air was crackling with the energy of love—true love, real love.

Chp. 39 "Glimpse of Gold"
"Behold thy salvation cometh; behold his reward is with him." [Isaiah 62:11]

Christian and Hope found the low wall and climbed back over. They had made it through The Enchanted Ground. It hadn't been easy. But it was all worth it, because now they could see, with the naked eye, their heavenly destination, a city indeed built of shiny pearls and precious stones. It was on the highest hill of any they had seen, and its winding, gold main street scintillated like a ribbon on a birthday gift heaven-sent. Christian and Hope hugged each other tightly, jumping joyfully up and down.

"It can't be more than half a day away," said Christian, beside himself with excitement.

"I think you're right, Christian!" beamed Hope. "I hope we will be there soon."

* * *

By this time, though, Christian and Hope remembered Igor, their on-again, off-again companion. "We've got to go back and help him," said Christian. "He'll cross to smell the flowers, then he'll never make it through; he's so slow."

"But we couldn't even make it through ourselves. There is no time. The angel told us to go. It's best left in the hands of the King," urged Hope.

Agitated, Christian called to Igor, but he was nowhere in sight.

* * *

The low walls of the path were now nothing but rocks placed sporadically along the way. The two moved along. They had had the rest that they needed for the energy that would be required in the final, most dangerous phase of their journey.

They arrived at a second set of lush, verdant vineyards and knew their dream of entering the Celestial City was about to become a reality. *Dear King,* Christian said in his mind, *thank you for your loving care today and so many other days of my life.*

Chp. 40 "At The River's Edge"

"When thou passest through the waters, I will be with thee, and through the rivers, they shall not overflow thee." *[Isaiah 43:2]*

Life in this part of the Delectable Mountains was easy and equable, not like the journey there. The weather was just perfect—mild and clear, and the walking was effortless. An idyllic, quaint little group of cottages appeared; it was picture-perfect with its curls of smoke wafting from the chimneys and children playing. Hope and Christian decided the scene being so lovely called for another rest. One of the children, intrigued, called to them to come sit on their porch, ran in to get his mama, and that is how it all began--folk from the village received the wanderers into their community with open arms, in fact the widest imaginable. They befriended them, did thoughtful things for them, and entertained them, telling them to relax and enjoy, that life was a gift from God! With their generosity and kindnesses, Christian now slowed down enough to actually experience quite a few low-key, peaceful days there.

Days passed, even, ordinary, and happy. Yet Igor still had not caught up. *Would he see it through? Would he ever be sincere?* It was Christian's only concern. Seeing that out-of-place wisp of worry plainly amidst the serenity of this wonderful place, the villagers consoled Christian, though, and any last trace of negativity gradually faded away. Besides, he was in love with Hope, afterall, and that meant just everything! Those were the days, the days in the vineyards, on top of the world, a sense of security wrapped around Christian like a sleeping bag by a cozy fire.

* * *

Then, one day, one awful day, something occurred that made the blood in Christian's veins turn cold.

He had received permission to borrow a cell phone. With it, he had called home.

He hadn't known what to expect. He hadn't known if there would even be a ring tone, if the city had already been destroyed.

He was greeted by the sound of his brother's voice. Christian was filling up with long-lost fraternal love, and he gushed out terms of endearment, many expressions of heartfelt affection. "I love you; I want to see you both. . ."

When the boy was strangely silent, Christian stopped.

"Christian, . . . Christian, I have something to tell you," said the brother.

"What is it, Adam?" asked Christian, upset to know, upset not to know.

Adam's next words would fall like the head of a plutonium hammer. "It's our mother, Chris." Adam waited, not wanting to be the bearer of bad tidings.

"Go on!" yelled Christian, the sinking feeling settling into his very bones.

"Our mother-- she has cancer, Chris. She's in the hospital now."

"OK," said Christian bravely. "So the doctors'll treat her, and she'll be out soon. Right? . . . Right?" He saw mental snapshots of himself as a little boy and his mother tending a cut, kissing a bruise. The images of caregiving caresses flooded back.

"Chris, she's dying. She's terminal."

"Oh, God, no!!!" Christian screamed, overtones vibrating. *Why her?* The question carved a deep cleft into the harmony of the mountains.

He let the phone drop and immediately wept and wailed in the most heart-wrenching, gut-wrenching way. His wretched outpouring took control.

* * *

When Hope flew to his side, he related the devastating news. "This is the only thing I've never had to deal with yet. And now I'm here, dealing with it."

If his grandfather had been there, he would have told him there's no escaping what may invisibly follow any of us, but he was lost to him, eons away.

So Christian paused, mournfully, dropping his head to Hope, then added a question he knew he should not have, a question the weight of which was so heavy, so blasphemous and terrible, it had no right to be asked. Each word tolled distinctly, like a nail being slowly but harshly driven into a coffin: "Whose -- idea -- was -- this?" He stammered it in fitful vehemence.

Then, without warning, his anger escalated to ultimate pitch. He lashed out to the nearest thing alive. He shoved Hope behind him, his pain sorely misdirected, misunderstood, and blasted out an answer to his own empty, heinous question. "It's *your* Lord's, Hope, your great and wonderful *Lord*'s! That's who!" He spat it sullenly, while Hope was standing motionless, not speaking, in shock.

Then, "How can He allow this?" came whimpering from out his quivering lips.

These five soft words would be his last.

*   *   *

Instead of the sympathy that friends could have shared, ghastly images would be Christian's constant companion for the next few days. Every attempt to help him by the villagers had ended in him pushing them away, just as he had with Hope. He was caught up, he was stuck; a great rift of inertia and gloom debilitated him. He had no Faith, he had no Hope nor love now, and he would soon have no Mother.

Time stood still. It may have been flowing for everyone else, but not for Christian. It was a hellish, abstract illusion, a horrendous mental wasteland, a thoughtless isolation devoid of any feeling.

But then the angels returned to tell them that they had to finish the journey. Because of Christian's psychic blockage, the heavenly message was able to reach Hope's ears only, and Christian almost missed it. "Time to cross the river," relayed Hope, whose eyes still held tears that would not drop. "We are to go together," she said bravely, her voice filled with the love of deepest friendship battling torments of inscrutable rejection.

So it was time; yet Christian couldn't grasp it. He merely followed, like a soulless gathering of cells, as Hope led on. Then, as the realization set in that they were in fact leaving the last vineyard, the scene of so much former joy, Christian felt a twinge of at least something--reluctance. *I can't leave now; I've got to get back to my mother.* Earthly cares incapacitated him, things he'd left undone.

As one thought bled into another and then another, Christian for a moment contemplated his own impending passage. He was terrified, avoidant to take any further step.

"You know, when I was a little girl, I almost left here once. In our backyard pool. I felt as if I had gone to heaven," Hope said, reading Christian's fears, trying to give him some comfort. "It wasn't scary or terrible at all . . . from what I can remember, it was quite beautiful."

Christian was hearing this remarkable story, but not absorbing. He spurned it. His mind was beset with all the emotions one must face when loss comes like a thief in the night.

"Look, Chris, you've still got me," Hope pleaded bitterly. "Don't tell me the situation's hopeless. Nothing ever is, with the King."

Christian just looked away.

* * *

Soon, Christian and Hope, their relationship still severed beyond repair, were at the riverbank. Hope was staring far to the other side. Christian was holding his head in his hands, his eyes seeing not the imaginary sharks that Apollyon could materialize at any moment, but only pure black behind the finality of human eyelids, the terror of permanent nothingness.

"I've got to go now, Christian. They're calling me. You've got to come too. They're telling us to come!" Hope waded into the water.

But Christian just couldn't go! He just couldn't do it! Christian fought with himself, this foe worse than any Apollyon could have ever been.

Finally, he held his breath and went forward, in sheer confusion. He began struggling immediately, thrashing in the river's great depth.

Hope, on the other hand, had her mind's eye on the image of Jesus walking on water, and was going to prevail.

Christian felt the strong current, and, although he could swim, the relentless force of the water was pulling him under, just like he thought it would.

Hope was walking forward, her feet firm on the riverbed each step. She was turning backwards, yelling to Christian. "Just as I thought, it's not deep! You can easily cross!" But she had forgotten the words of Knowledge, who had hinted that individuals would find the depth different, depending on the level of their faith.

Christian desperately fought to keep his head above water. *There's no bottom!* he silently screamed. *It's so deep!* His mind was draining away all former strength. It felt like being in the middle of the ocean, stranded, weak.

"No, it's shallow! Just have Hope!" she shouted, reading his mind. "Your Faith is alive, close by, just on the other side, and your family loves you too!"

She continued shouting. But Christian was drowning. His lack of Faith, Hope, and love made for no foundation.

"You can do it! You can conquer it, Christian, if you just believe! Remember how you used to believe? Remember! Remember!!"

But Christian kept slipping beneath the water. For him, it was a whirlpool. His lungs were filling with water. His eyes were rolling back in his head, and his arms were slowing like a clock winding down at a deathbed. Hope grabbed at him to pull him up, but he fell through her arms, time and time again.

It didn't look like he was going to be capable.

Chp. 41 "So Close"

"If it tarry, wait for it, because it will surely come, and will not tarry." [Habukkuk 2:3]

Hope began to cry, because the unthinkable was happening: she was losing him, she was losing him. *It doesn't make sense!* she thought, out of her mind. She gasped as she watched his head sink down into the cold, crystal-clear depths, into the deep, deep water that ironically felt so fine to her.

The hair was flying upward, undulating. The right arm was extended upwards, the hand clenched in a position as if to scream *Help me!* The outline of the face wobbled a few times till it was six feet under.

"I can't help you enough!" cried Hope, screaming at the figure, lowering, lowering.

And then it simply disappeared, with nothing more. She looked away in bitter defeat.

She was sobbing harder than she ever had. "But love never fails! And I *loved* him!" she hurled up into the sky.

"Please C-Christian, come back! You were so close! So close!. . ." The tears that had never dropped before . . .finally. . . released.

"After all we've come through, after all we've done.. . . don't leave me now! . . She sat on the pebbly shore, rocking herself, moaning. "So close,. . . so c-close

. . . ." She was barely getting the broken words out, drowning in her own tortured, abysmal despair, repeating herself, then finally fading, fainting. Her spirit was departing, though precariously; she wasn't tasting her own victory. Something was terribly wrong.

* * *

But that wasn't how she left the Earth, nor how Christian died-- hopeless, faithless, and loveless-- alone and at the bottom of a river. No, it wasn't that way at all! You see, as Christian was sinking for the final time, he had put aside his anger, grief, and doubt and called on the name of Jesus, be it ever so weakly. If his call could have taken up space, it would have been no bigger than the size of a mustard seed, an infinitesimally small speck, a molecule of water. But the King heard it and responded with enough love to cover all Christian's weaknesses.

And that is all it takes! An invisible hand reached down from the atmosphere into the water and grasped Christian's arm firmly. It pulled him up.

Then angels whisked the old shells of the hardhearted Christian and the heartbroken Hope away and carried them together through the air, up a hill.

They were flying above the clouds now, melting towards a feeling of transcendent peace beyond all earthy care. It was just a moment before the spirit inside of them quickened and their eyes reflected a new, divine spark.

* * *

They moved furiously through a different dimension of time and space now, something inexplicable, ineffable in human terms. Enveloped in a tunnel of light, Christian and Hope clung to the angels as if they were babies clutching their parents in an inseparable bond of love.

Telepathically, the spirits were giving them a vivid

description of their new home, of what the Celestial City was going to be like. It went way beyond what they had seen through the telescope, or ever imagined.

"No pain?" asked Christian. "Ever again?"

"No pain ever again," came the answer.

"No worry, no disappointment?"

"No worry, no disappointment," said an angel.

"No discomfort, nor hunger?"

"No discomfort nor hunger."

"No lying, no murder, no hate, . . .no betrayal or evil?" he pressed, thinking it was all too good to be true. "No earthquakes, no storms? No faltering, yearning, nor strife?"

"None, my dear, none."

Christian paused, and then built up the courage to ask his final troublesome question. "No disease?" he asked feebly.

"Best of all, NO disease!" affirmed an angel. "Only abundant health and happiness, borne out of unconditional, permanent, all-encompassing love," he said. "That's what the fabric of His kingdom is made of."

The heavenly beings said that it would be very soon now, that the young man and woman were passing away, entering a whole new existence.

Chp. 42 "For Thine is The Kingdom, the Power, and the Glory, Forever"

"That for these things' sake the wrath of God cometh upon the children of disobedience." [Ephesians 5:6]

When Christian reached the entrance to the kingdom of the Celestial City, in the arms of the angels, it was everything and more than he had ever hoped it could be. Walking with his beloved Hope arm in arm, they approached the resplendent gate, studded with pearls, and a mighty gathering of angels came out to join them through a burst of light. Triumphant trumpet blasts filled the sweet air. Stripes of the most indescribably exquisite, rich hues, the likes of which we have never seen on earth, magically banded together to create rainbows, scattered among the soft clouds on the ground of the lofty mountain peak.

Christian and Hope were then asked for their certificates, and they most gladly complied. One heavenly spirit examined the rolls, then nodded his approval. Christian and Hope were transfigured into holy angels, and were officially welcomed in through the gate of Heaven, while the music of choruses of cherubim and seraphim on high resounded throughout the spheres.

Before the door of the gate was to close, though, some events occurred that are of interest to anyone who aspires to go to the Celestial City. For one thing, all the mysteries ever thought of were answered; everything became completely clear—including the suffering and the particular lessons of what had been needed. But even better, the spirits of several individuals they had known on Earth were waiting.

First came forward a little boy whom Christian had never met, but who held a teddy bear and came running up to hug him and thank him for his thoughts on the first huge hill.

Next came the man whom he had mistakenly left for dead, crushed in the valley of squalid shacks. The man was smiling and repeating, "I forgive you. I forgive you. . . It is nothing now. Evil can never touch us. Thank you for telling me."

Evan was there too, rejoicing for the spirits' safe return. "I got here just a little before you. I told you it was real!" he exuded, drawing Christian to him.

"Yes," said Christian, you were the first to tell me about the Way, and for that I can never repay you."

Then Christian saw the long, beautiful blonde hair he had missed for so long. It was Faith. "We were brought back together when you spoke His name in the river, sweet Christian. You had found me again not now, but then," she said, cradling his head with her cheek tightly to his.

Last, Christian's beloved grandfather advanced towards him slowly, his arms outstretched, his eyes and smile glowing with the essence of pure love, his tattered, old Bible in his hands. "You found it! You found it!" declared Christian, the new angel, who embraced the old man's spirit form with all that he had.

But best of all, the King of the land, Jesus Christ himself, in all his radiant glory, handsome, intelligent, and powerful beyond all compare, was there to reunite with each of them. He met Hope first, then Christian, while Hope and Faith, beloved soul-sisters, went off together to become re-acquainted.

Christian went to bow in deference, but the King picked him up off the floor and held him in the most wonderful embrace of all.

"Savior, oh Savior!" panted Christian.

In return, the Savior acted as if He had been pining for Christian for thousands of years, and ordered his angels to make ready for a grand, elaborate celebration, the details of which are impossible to list.

"Well done, my good and faithful servant," He said with a voice that obliterated the strangle-hold of all former earthly chains and permeated every fiber of Christian's new being. Christ received Christian home with so much boundless love that the light could be seen for miles, perhaps galaxies, away—identifiable if one really knew what was being looked at. It was a perfect union, thought Christian, meant for souls who truly believed.

That was all anyone had ever really needed.

"Make ready, Christian, your mother comes now," said his grandfather.

* * *

Rodney, beginning to detach from his dream, got a small, brief glimpse of the city inside the gate, just as its gleaming bars were closing. There were many angels, spirits of Earth's departed souls. Rodney Middleton wished himself among them.

Two seconds before Rodney was to wake up, though, he saw Igor running up the mount to the Celestial City, having finally caught up. When asked for his certificate, however, the ignorant Igor could not produce one. He was flown away by the angel Sincerity, left at the sulfurous hole in the hill that awaited the reckless or indecisive.

Rodney twitched in terror as he sat bolt upright in bed.

The End.